The COMMON QUEST

"... for the larger view will guide us
as we join in common quest."

John Andrew Storey

The COMMON QUEST

*Selected writings of
John Andrew Storey*

Edited by
Charles Hughes and Sylvia Storey

The Lindsey Press
London

©
Charles Hughes and Sylvia Storey
2000

ISBN 0 853 19 063 1

Published by
The Lindsey Press
1-6 Essex Street
London WC2R 3HY

Printed and bound in the United Kingdom by
J. W. Arrowsmith Ltd., Bristol

PREFACE

At some stage in our lives, perhaps quite suddenly in response to some defining moment or crisis, perhaps more gradually with advancing years, each one of us is likely to find himself or herself asking a question: "What, if any, is the meaning, or purpose, of my life?"

Some may already have a ready answer provided by a faith. But many may experience difficulty in accepting one. Thus, they may become seekers.

This little book records the results of one person who questioned his original faith and became a seeker, an "adventure of the spirit" if you like.

When the time may come for you too to be a seeker, this book may then serve as a companion in your quest, a common one.

John Andrew Storey
1935-1997

CONTENTS

INTRODUCTION

It is apparent that, over a period of roughly twelve years during his college years and early ministries, John Storey underwent a period of intense questioning and seeking. By the time that he began to publish, around his mid thirties, his views and interests — and they were many, as we shall see — were already shaped into a well constructed edifice. It seems logical and appropriate, therefore, not to follow a strict chronological order in material, but to present it by topics.

His written material includes not only some forty-odd hymns but also seventy-seven articles, comprising essays, poems, reviews and prayers, contributed to *The Inquirer* over a time span from 1969 to 1997, together with a comparable quantity of material in other miscellaneous publications. Also available are some unpublished manuscripts, including a long review of Zen Buddhism and other essays, texts of sermons and addresses, and a book of aphorisms (Li Shu K'ung below).

A selection has clearly had to be made from this material. Fortunately, the volume of material is sufficient to ensure adequate coverage in each of the topic chapters below.

The date of each item is recorded wherever possible in the attribution. Sometimes an article appears in more than one journal, in which case the attribution is given to the earlier one, except for the hymns which carry an attribution to the different hymnbooks in which they may occur. Where an article has appeared more than once in different issues of the same journal, attribution is made to the later one if the article is in a revised version.

Universalism

In the first two items, John provides us with a forthright definition on this, the core of his philosophy, followed by an autobiographical sketch published in the year of his death. *Twin Pillars*, the earliest of all John's published writings included here, is especially interesting because it reflects his period of seeking and expresses some seed-thoughts. It questions the basis of religion, refers to the Buddhist approach, and emphasises individual conscience, "that small voice within", however one may choose to define it. It is also interesting to note the great range of sources referred to in *Many Religions* and *The Golden Rule*. The chapter concludes with a hymn, a short poem, and three prayers.

Meditation
John Storey attached very great importance to this as an avenue to spiritual health. He has noted elsewhere that societies which we may tend, superciliously and ignorantly, to dismiss as primitive, such as the Aborigines of Australia, spend a significant proportion of their disposable time in meditation. The I*ntroduction to Meditation* is an extremely useful guide for those who may be unfamiliar with technique. One could very well add the *Eightfold Path of Buddhism* (see below) to the themes that could profitably be considered for meditation.

Buddhism
This chapter became the longest in the book for a very good reason: The Buddhist approach to religion epitomises that of John Storey. John's sympathy with Buddhism has ensured that the four excerpts from *Introduction to Buddhist Teaching* presented here read extremely well, and provide a very fine and lucid introduction to the subject. All one can say to anyone seriously wishing to consider following the path that John has trod is that the material of this chapter deserves the very closest study and thought.

Nature and Ecology
Each one of us, one suspects, has experienced some unforgettable moments of contact with Nature. Several emotions are inevitably aroused: First is an appreciation of the beauty and majesty of Nature. This can be akin to a deep religious experience. Then may follow a determination to preserve this great spectacle and heritage for the future. All this is eloquently covered by John, who includes appropriate references to Chief Seattle's immortal words and the lovely Tewa Indian *Song of the Loom*.

A Calendar
In these articles, all but one based on important events in the Christian calendar, John shares his thoughts on the significance of each for him personally.

Peace
As opposed to the knee-jerk response, deep in the human psyche, to the call of "patriotism", alas so easily exploitable, John gently reminds us that there may be a higher duty, in pursuing which the answer lies within ourselves.

Hymns
John Andrew Storey will always be remembered for his hymns. Not only was he to become easily the most prolific Free Church hymn-writer of the late 20th century, but the inspiration of these hymns came to include a great variety of sources in addition to conventional Christian ones - a truly universalist approach. John contributed 23 hymns to the two modern American hymnals *Singing the Living Tradition* and *How Can We keep From Singing!* and no less than 32 to the British *Hymns For Living.*

The words of six hymns, where they happen to be particularly relevant, have been included in other chapters of this book. A further selection of nine hymns is included here. In passing, one notes the universalist aspect of John's hymns, sources for which include, in addition to familiar Biblical and Christian themes, the following: the Ancient Egyptian *Book of the Dead*, Akhnaton, Confucius, Socrates, Buddhist Scriptures, a verse by Omar Khayyam, a 19th century Chinese poem, and the Dalai Lama!

The two short excerpts at the end of this chapter are from a short address given by John during a concert featuring a visiting American Junior High School Choir. The first provides a glimpse of John's humour, the second is a profound comment on the importance of hymns. Taken in context, it is obvious that John's remarks were entirely appropriate to the occasion, and that all those participating would have taken away a pleasant and useful memory of them. With typical modesty, John makes reference not to himself but to a fellow hymn-writer.

Haiku
These are concise and attractive in their own right. John reminds us, moreover, that it is important to look at that "to which the finger points" rather than the verse itself, and that there is an inherent spiritual element in Haiku closely akin to Zen Buddhism.

Sayings of Li Shu K'ung
John clearly enjoyed composing these delightful "Confucian" aphorisms. Among his effects is a little notebook devoted to them alone, containing no less than 97 of them neatly written out and organised, as here, into sections. In writing for parish magazines and the like, John had at times employed the noms-de-plume "John Fenman" and "Ann Drew" whose derivation is obvious. The origin of this third nom-de-plume, Li Shu K'ung, is a little enigmatic.

A Chinese friend, Dr. Yan Jing Wang, a Chinese doctor now practising medicine in Cambridge, whose first degree was in Ancient Chinese literature, has said that Li Shu (or, more commonly, Shu Li) is merely a common Chinese name, just as common say as John is in English. Of K'ung he said that it is a difficult word to translate but offered the following series of comments on it: 'Life is for a short time' . . . 'it comes and goes' . . . 'no one knows why, or can foretell, tragedy or disaster' . . . 'only life knows' . . . 'only God knows' . . . 'God is life' . . . 'if someone knows [accepts?] K'ung, then life follows "naturally"'. Clearly therefore this nom-de-plume of John's is meant to signify something like "John the philosopher", expressed in a typically modest way.

Speaking Out
These articles demonstrate how anyone who has thought things out for himself or herself becomes morally obliged to take a stance on issues which may well be considered controversial, politically or otherwise.

Reflections on Childhood
These are gentle essays, all written during John's brief retirement years. They each have a moral and, in addition, throw some light on John's formative years.

Epilogue
This chapter contains not only some of the most hauntingly beautiful of John's poetry, but also some of his deepest thoughts. Poignantly, nearly all the items included here were written during the last years of his life. They surely speak for themselves, and indeed it is now high time to let John Storey speak to us.

UNIVERSALISM

The Universalist Approach

There is more than one meaning to the word "Universalist". I shall use it solely to indicate one who seeks wisdom and inspiration from all the great religions and philosophies of the world and who does not give her/his allegiance exclusively to any one faith.

. . . One does not reverence Christ any the less because one has learned to respect other Teachers and Prophets also. Christianity has always been a most important component in my universalist faith. It will remain so. But it will be a Christianity which has been both enriched and modified by other insights.

The Inquirer, No.7143, 8 November 1986.

*   *   *   *   *   *   *

> Our faith is but a single gem
> Upon a rosary of beads . . .

Opening lines of *All Faiths*, Hymn Number 130 in *Hymns for Living*. 1985.

Universalism

Even when I was still, officially, an orthodox Christian I had strong universalist leanings. As a student training for the Congregational ministry, my favourite subject was comparative religion, one of the subjects in which I always got top marks in all the exams. I was lucky in having a tutor who really knew his subject and always made it interesting. His approach was always liberal, and he was very tolerant in his treatment of the non-Christian religions. This pleased me, but not all the students. We not only learned about Eastern religions and philosophies, but we looked at what the West has to offer. We learned about the Stoics, Christian mystics and, what really interested me, the North American Indians and their rich spiritual life.

I think it was while looking at the Indians that I first became interested in the Universalist Church of America, which, like the Quakers, always treated the Indians fairly. It was about this time that I first made contact with Unitarians, and learned about their close connection with the Universalist Church. In fact the two American bodies united in 1961 and became the UUA. It was becoming obvious to me that there would have to be some changes in my life.

Those who knew me well could see the way things were going, and were not a bit surprised when I became a Unitarian. I never make any secret of the fact that it was the Universalist stand that was the main attraction. Some of my friends wondered if I would have any regrets, and I sometimes wondered that myself. Over the years there have been some disappointments. But the publication of the excellent *Hymns for Living* which so fairly represents all shades of Unitarian opinion, including Universalism, did much to restore my faith.

I am no longer in the active ministry, having had to take an early retirement on health grounds because of my slowly worsening MS. When I retired I moved to Dorset, a county where Unitarian churches are very thin on the ground. Quaker meetings are more in evidence, and I soon found my local meeting where I was made very welcome. There I learned about the

Quaker Universalist Group which believes that spiritual awareness is accessible to men and women of any religion or none,
and that no one faith can claim to be a final revelation or to have
a monopoly of truth. The group is open to both Quakers and
non-Quakers and I soon became a member. The group publish-
es an excellent journal called *The Universalist* to which I sometimes make contributions.

I also learned about the Quaker practice of dual member-
ship of the Society of Friends without having to leave one's
present church. Perhaps the best known dual member is Canon
Paul Oestreicher, Canon of Coventry Cathedral. He is not the
only one by any means. I have decided to apply for dual mem-
bership as I am sure that this is the right thing for me. Theolog-
ically I shall always be a Unitarian. And I am certain I will
always be a Universalist.

The Inquirer, No.7408, 4 January 1997.

*   *   *   *   *   *   *

A Universalist Prayer

O thou that art, though mankind calls thee by a hundred names,
thou art beyond all human telling, and though we seek thee here
thou art everywhere to be found. All our many faiths are but
partial expressions of thy Presence, and our many names for
thee reflect the countless aspects of thy Being. What can we say
of thee, save that *Thou Art*, and that by thy Presence around us
and within we are sustained? As the earth is to the growing
plant, and the water to the thirsty land, so art thou to us. As vital
as the air we breathe, so is thy Presence in our lives. Thou dost
not need the simple words we offer, and it is for our good alone
that we give thee praise. Therefore do we praise thee now, and
in so doing fulfil our deepest needs.

Devotional Life, No.54, supplement to *Faith and Freedom*, No.108,
Summer 1983.

The Twin Pillars

The importance of a good foundation in building is well known. It is true, too, that in societies and organisations of every description a sound basis is needed. This is especially true of religion. But upon what is religion to be based? Many answers have been given, but I like that of the Buddhists — from whom I believe we have much to learn — for they claim that their religion is based on the twin pillars of wisdom and compassion. It is not my intention to examine if their claim is true, though I believe it is, but to suggest that we might well adopt this idea for ourselves and seek to base our religion upon these twin pillars. Both pillars are needed, for the one without the other cannot support the whole edifice of religion. Even Bertrand Russell said that "the good life is one inspired by love and guided by knowledge", and if you substitute wisdom for knowledge I would agree.

I would draw this distinction between wisdom and knowledge, for although the two often go together they are quite distinct.

The wise man keeps his mouth closed and his mind open. He is a good listener, yet not easily swayed by argument one way or the other. He is not impressed by the one who shouts the loudest, nor does he follow blindly in the crowd. He approaches each problem with an open mind, unmoved by threats or bribes, unimpeded by pre-conceived notions and prejudices. He weighs up all sides of the case, sifts the evidence, considers what the consequences will be if he takes this course, or what they will be if he takes that course. He considers not only the immediate effects, but the long term implications. He subjects everything to the careful process of thought and meditation and he makes no hasty judgement.

He listens to that small voice within, which some call "the voice of reason" and others "the voice of God", but which in either case is the divine whisper.

But wisdom needs to find an outlet, needs to express itself in a practical way, and this is where we come to compassion —

the other great pillar upon which religion rests. It is hardly necessary for me to remind you that in all the great religions of the world love is extolled as the most important thing.

Unfortunately, the word love has become very much debased in recent times. We talk of loving ice-cream or loving television, when all that we really mean is that we like these things. Often the word love is used when the word lust would be more appropriate. This is why I much prefer the word compassion which as yet is not debased in this way. It suggests passionate caring. It suggests a complete and utter giving of oneself, unconditionally. It carries with it the suggestion of sacrifice in the service of others which is very far removed from the sickly sentimental love of the popular song.

So important is this idea of compassion in the religions of the world, that some would have us make it the be-all and end-all of religion. Yet I do not think we can do that, for as with all great forces, compassion needs careful handling and direction. It has got to be guided by wisdom. We have all seen the consequences of love that is not guided by wisdom.

Wisdom and compassion, noble pillars indeed upon which can rest the whole edifice of religion. It is upon these twin pillars that I would like to see our religion based, indeed all religion based, for it is along these lines that I would hope to see a growing measure of unity among all religious people.

The creeds, dogmas and doctrines of religion are divisive, they separate man from man and nation from nation. Now, more than ever, the peoples of the world have got to learn to live together. Religion, more than anything else can help to accomplish this, but only if the religions of the world drop their doctrinaire attitudes and cease to make their exclusive claims. Differences there will always be, nor should this concern us overmuch. Nor will it, if our own faith is based firmly on those noble twin pillars, Wisdom and Compassion.

World Faiths, No.64, September 1965.

Many Religions

Universalism began, not as a revolt against the Trinity, as did Unitarianism, but in opposition to the harsh doctrine that only the elect in mankind will be saved. As opposed to the doctrine taught by fundamentalist Christians that only those who accept Christ as their personal saviour will be saved, the Universalists taught "Universal Salvation" — that is that all people would be saved no matter to which religion they belonged. From this broad-minded and tolerant view there grew up among them a profound interest in other religions, and in time the recognition that their loyalty could not be confined to Christianity exclusively but that it was their duty to accept and proclaim, acknowledge and learn from the truths of all great religions.

Religion, sad to say, has all too often been the cause of division and misunderstanding. In these dangerous times when co-operation and brotherhood are needed among the peoples of the world as never before, we cannot afford to take the narrow or intolerant view. Universalism is a beautiful and noble concept. It suggests a wide view, a broad and deep understanding, an all embracing love. Christians delight to call each other "brothers and sisters in Christ", and it is excellent that they should see each other in that light. Still more wonderful is the attitude of the Universalist who can regard all men of goodwill as his brethren, and who can embrace with open arms all honest seekers after truth no matter to which religion they belong.

Unpublished manuscript.

*   *   *   *   *   *   *

Mankind is One; all are leaves of one tree, flowers in one garden. Religion must be the cause of love and harmony, else it is no religion.

Baha'i Scriptures

Altar flowers are of many species, but all Worship is one; Systems of Faith are different, but God is One.

Hindu Scriptures

My House shall be called a House of Prayer for all Peoples.

Hebrew Scriptures

He who is beloved of the Lord honours every form of Religious Faith.

Buddhist Scriptures

Make thyself pure, O righteous man! Any one in the world here below can win purity for himself when he cleanses himself with Good Thoughts, Good Words and Good Deeds.

Parsee Scriptures

Recognise him as holy in whom are found friendship, sympathy and pleasure at the welfare of others ... When man meeteth the Friend, he obtaineth happiness. O God, Thou art the Friend. Thou art wise. It is Thou who unitest men with Thee.

Sikh Scriptures

Men have rent their great concern into sects, every party rejoicing in that which is their own. Wherefore, leave them until a certain time. One day God will call to them and say 'Where are my companions?' And He will bring up a witness out of every nation and say: 'Bring your proofs.' And they shall know that Truth is with God alone . . . To his own book shall every nation be called . . . And thou shalt see every nation kneeling.

The Holy Qur'an

One is your Father and all too are Brethren ...God is no respecter of persons, but in every nation he that revereth Him and worketh righteousness is accepted of Him . . . for He hath made of One Blood all the nations of the earth.

Christian Scriptures

The Unitarian, No.934, October 1981, p.93

The Golden Rule

Compassion and benevolence are intrinsically bound up with The Golden Rule which is found in all the great religions of the World, expressed either in its positive or negative form.

*   *   *   *   *   *   *

Tsze-kung asked, "Is there one word which may serve as a rule of practice for all one's life?" The Master replied, "Is not 'reciprocity' such a word? What you do not want done to yourself, do not do unto others."

The Analects of Confucius

The Way of the Measuring Square:
> What a man dislikes in those above him,
> He must not bring to bear on those beneath him.
> What he dislikes in those beneath him,
> He must not bring to the service of those above him.
> What he dislikes in his forebears,
> He must not do in advance for his descendants.
> What he would dislike is his descendants,
> He must not do as following his forebears.
> What he dislikes to receive on the right,
> Let him not bestow on the left;
> And what he dislikes to receive on the left,
> Let him not bestow on the right.
> This is what is meant by the Way of the Measuring Square.
> The Great Learning (Confucian Classic)

No one of you is a believer until he loves for his brother what he loves for himself.

Moslem Traditional Writings

This is the sum of all true righteousness,
Treat others as you would yourself be treated.
Do nothing to your neighbour which hereafter
You would not have your neighbour do unto you.
In causing pleasure, or in giving pain,
In doing good or injury to others,
In granting or refusing a request,
A man obtains a proper rule of action
By regarding his neighbour as himself.

Mahabharata

Therefore all things whatsoever ye would that men should do to you, do ye even so to them for this is the law and the prophets.

Matthew 7:12, Luke 6:31

Thou shalt love thy neighbour as thyself.

Matthew 19:19, Romans 13:9, Galatians 5:14

The Golden Rule is reinforced by Jesus as the second of the Two Great Commandments.

Matthew 22:39, Mark 12:31, Luke 10.27

Note: A Conference of religious educationalists was held at Manchester College Oxford in 1978 to seek for common ground between world religions in School Assembly Worship. The Conference found that the one basic religious teaching upon which all the world faiths were in complete agreement was The Golden Rule.

Devotional Life, No.51, supplement to *Faith and Freedom*, No.105, Summer 1982.

All Earth's Children

For all the paths which guide our ways
We lift our hearts in joyful praise.
For Akhenaton, by whose hand
New light was brought to Egypt's land.
For Moses, and Judaic seers,
And every Hebrew psalm which cheers.
For Jesus Christ of lowly birth,
Who sought to found God's reign on earth:

For Hindu's varied paths to God
Which many noble souls have trod.
For Buddha's path, which, like the Jain,
Has shown the way to conquer pain.
For Guru Nanak, Punjab's son,
And all that noble Sikhs have done.
For Japanese and Chinese lore,
Confucian wisdom, Shinto awe.

For Zarathustra, Parsi sage,
The fount of Persia's golden age.
For Islam's Prophet, who by grace
Transformed a wayward desert race.
For Stoic souls of Rome and Greece,
Whose fame on earth shall never cease.
For all great souls, with common voice,
Let all earth's children now rejoice!

How Can We Keep From Singing! 1976, Number 86.
Hymns for Living, 1985, Number 131.

Let a Hundred Flowers Bloom

Let a hundred flowers
together bloom;
In the one garden there is room
for all to flourish,
nourished by the same showers.
And we should know
that in the garden of mankind
may grow
in harmony the flowers of the mind.

The Universalist, No.50, June 1997.

* * * * * * *

Three Prayers

Father of all mankind, teach us that our many religions are but the different colours into which thy pure white light of truth is broken in its passage through the prism of our finite minds.

O God, teach us the wisdom of tolerance, that we may never forget that he who maliciously speaks evil of another's Faith. thereby injures the good name of his own.

Help us, O Lord, to see that our own Religion is but one jewel on a necklace, and that through all Faiths there runs the divine thread of thy ineffable Truth.

The Inquirer, No.6658, 21 February 1970.

SAYINGS OF LI-SHU-K'UNG

The Way of Religion

Wherein lies the nature of true religion? Is it not in the searching after truth and in having compassion for all beings?

As a starving person gratefully accepts food from any hand, so does the person who is hungry for knowledge accept truth from any source.

Greediness for most things may be a vice, but greediness for truth is always a virtue.

With many people religion is like mountain snow. On the heights away from the people it maintains its purity; when brought into the heat of life it melts away.

Being religious consists not in the observations of holy days, but in the living of holy lives.

As the bee takes nectar from many flowers and makes of it the one substance of honey, so does the wise person take truth from all religions and make of it the one substance of faith.

Men ask concerning the respective merits of Lao-Tsu, Confucius and the Buddha. Would not a wise man accept three lanterns to lighten his path on a dark night rather than one?

MEDITATION

A Prayer

O Inner Being, who art hidden within the human heart as the fragrance is hidden within the flower, we would contemplate in reverence the wonder of thy universal presence. We see thy beauty hidden in all lovely things, thy love in all kindly deeds, thy goodness in all noble lives. May we learn also to see thee in the common things of life, even in those things which to the unenlightened eye do not seem beautiful or good, and in those people of whom we are tempted to think but little. Above all, may we so learn to live our lives that others may see something of thee in us.

> May the Inner Light shine through us
> illuminating for others the road of life.

From *With Hands Together II*, Lindsey Press, 1993.

The Depths of Inner Space

Once the fearless navigator
Sailing from some native shore,
Bravely crossed uncharted waters,
Finding new lands to explore.

Now we look beyond our planet,
Reaching upward to the stars;
We have walked the lunar deserts —
Soon we'll tread the soil of Mars.

All that science may discover,
As the Universe it delves,
Will be only scraps of knowledge,
If we fail to know ourselves.

So the journey of the spirit,
Which each human soul must face,
Takes us on a greater voyage,
To the depths of inner space.

Hymns for Living, 1985, Number 40.
Previously as "Know Thyself" in *How Can We Keep From Singing!*
1976, Number 132.

*   *   *   *   *   *   *

Remember, O seeker,
This truth divine,
The Light is within thee,
Let the Light shine!

A Benediction from the Egyptian Heirophants (verse rendering by
J.A.S).

Introduction to Meditation

I might begin by asking a question: "Why should we meditate?" Put briefly, the answer is, I think: "Because we need to!" It has been said that unless humans can find sufficient wisdom to match their increasing knowledge, their history could well end in disaster. The acquisition of knowledge leads to cleverness, which is not necessarily a virtue! The practice of meditation leads to wisdom. Hence the importance of meditation in the world today. Man is by nature an explorer, but as a widely-travelled man once remarked, "Only the inward journey is real." That inward journey is what meditation is all about.

In commenting briefly on the practice of meditation I must firstly draw your attention to the importance of giving due regard to the practical little details. Experience has shown that the best results are obtained when one sticks to a set time and place. The body should be poised and alert, yet relaxed and comfortable. The lotus position — the cross-legged position on the floor — is advised for those who can learn it without discomfort, but this is not a matter of fundamental importance. Having taken a comfortable position, one must then relax oneself completely, and this is best done by breathing slowly and deeply from the stomach. This relaxes the body while at the same time it helps to stimulate the mind.

To obtain the maximum benefit from meditation one should first develop the powers of concentration. A sportsman knows that he will do no good on the field of play until he has first of all tuned up his body and developed his muscles. To this end he will devote himself to hours of physical exercise. In the same way little is gained from meditation until one has first developed his or her 'mental muscles'. This is done by learning to concentrate, and most manuals on meditation give lists of exercises which help to this end.

Concentration on the breathing process is one such exercise. Inhale through the nostrils normally, without strain, without force. Mentally count one. Exhale and count two. Inhale and count three. Count up to ten constantly concentrating on the breathing process without thinking of anything else. When you get to ten, start a new series beginning at one. Gradually you may increase the number of series. My own opinion is that for those who wish to sharpen their powers of concentration before taking up the practice of mediation in earnest, a few minutes a day spent in concentration exercises will probably bring results better than an hour's practice once a week.

Once one has passed the preliminary stages of learning how to concentrate, then longer sessions of the practice of meditation proper become desirable, since little of real worth is achieved from a meditation session of less than half an hour. From the point of view of meditation, then, one really good session a week — say, of at least forty-five minutes — will produce better results than a few minutes a day could do. Where little time is available from one's busy daily routine, this is better spent in trying to keep in trim one's 'mental muscles' with some simple concentration exercises than in trying to embark upon a serious attempt at meditation which, through lack of time, is almost certain to be disappointing.

Opinions differ among meditators as to the desirability of setting oneself in advance a theme on which to meditate. For those who prefer this, the choice of 'seed-thought' — the object for meditation — has infinite possibilities. One may choose to meditate upon some particular doctrine of religion, or some passage of scripture. One's subject may be a verse or a saying, or even something one has heard in a sermon! You may choose to meditate on certain facts of life, the immensity of the Universe, the complexity of life in all its forms, that everything in existence — oneself included — is in a constant state of flux undergoing ceaseless change. Or again, the subject may be one of the great virtues. Love provides an excellent subject for meditation.

First try to wash from the mind all impurities, lust, hatred and ignorance, and endeavour to suffuse your own being with unbounded love. Then turn your thoughts to a friend and try to direct the same thoughts of love toward him or her. Then turn your feelings upon someone to whom you are indifferent. Next, and most difficult, visualise an enemy or someone whom you dislike, and even though at first it is difficult to do so without a feeling of hypocrisy, pervade him or her with the warmth of generous affection. Finally, radiate loving-kindness to all mankind, and so through all the Universe.

Though the practice of meditation is rapidly growing in the West — a trend which I heartily welcome — there are still those who regard the whole business with suspicion, seeing it as little more than an act of spiritual self-indulgence which confers no benefits and which has little to do with the hard world of reality. Yet in truth the practice of meditation is of the highest practical value and is a prerequisite for all real service, for only as we become the true masters of ourselves can we become the true servants of others. Practising meditation is like cleaning windows, so that the light that is within you may illumine the path around you, that others may see the light and tread more surely the path. As I said right at the beginning, in the time available we can only scratch the surface of this deep and complex subject. Yet little though it may be that we have learned, it is sufficient to enable us to make a beginning. Even the longest journey begins with a single step, and we can take that at least. Even the acquisition of a little wisdom can work wonders, for as we learn in the Sutra of Wei Lang:

> "even as the light of a lamp can break up darkness which has been there for a thousand years, so can a spark of wisdom do away with ignorance which has lasted for ages."

The light is there to be found, but so often we turn our back to the light and complain about the shadow in front. To those who doubt their ability there is but one word — TRY! And in meditation, as in all things, there are but two basic rules: begin and continue!

The Inquirer, No.6722, 19 August 1972.

Nameless Presence

As vital as the air I need,
As infinite as endless space,
The life within the smallest seed,
Your presence everywhere I trace.

Beyond the range of mortal speech,
In vain my prayers I try to frame,
Yet still my spirit yearns to reach
The Mystery it cannot name.

The Inquirer, No.6905, 24 September 1977.

*   *   *   *   *   *   *

WORDS TO INTRODUCE SILENT MEDITATION

Let us each pass through our own private door
and enter that secret place,
where alone,
we meet with our God
and find acceptance.
Be still,
and know your God is there.

Devotional Life, No.50, supplement to *Faith and Freedom*, No.104, Spring 1982

Meditation on The Indwelling Presence

This meditation can be used for corporate worship or for private devotions. The quotations should be read slowly with long pauses between for reflection.

In the Book of the Prophet Jeremiah we read: This is the Covenant I will make saith the Lord: I will put my law in their inward parts, and in their hearts will I write it.

Robert Browning said: There is an inward centre in ourselves where truth abides in fullness.

St. Augustine said: Return within yourselves, for it is within the inward man that truth dwells.

Plato wrote in The Republic: Every one had better be ruled by divine wisdom dwelling within him.

The Apostle Paul said: Know ye not that ye are the temple of God, and that the Spirit of God dwelleth within you.

The Bhagavad-Gita reminds us: God is seated in the hearts of all.

From the Tibetan Scripture "The Voice of the Silence" we learn that: Before the Soul can see, the harmony within must be attained, and fleshly eyes be blind to all illusion.

I*n the Granth, Holy Book of the Sikhs, we read:* God is in thy heart, yet thou searchest for him in the wilderness.

The Unitarian hymn writer, F. L. Hosmer, tells us: The outward God he findeth not, who finds not God within.

Devotional Life, No.42, supplement to *Faith and Freedom*, No.96, Summer 1979.

Meditation on Loving Kindness

First think of your heart and mind being cleansed of all anger, ill-will, cruelty, jealousy, envy, passion and aversion.

Seek to awaken within yourself the desire that your mind should be pure, free from all impurities; free from lust, hatred and ignorance; free from all evil thoughts.

Think to yourself: "My mind is now pure and clean - like a polished mirror."

As a clean and empty vessel is filled with pure water, now fill your clean heart and pure mind with peaceful and sublime thoughts of boundless loving-kindness, overflowing compassion, sympathetic joy and perfect equanimity.

Now think to yourself "My whole body is saturated with loving-kindness and compassion. I have sublimated myself, elevated myself, ennobled myself."

Mentally create an aura of loving-kindness around you. You are now a fortress and a stronghold of morality.

You should now be able to say: "I return good for evil, loving kindness for anger, compassion for cruelty, sympathetic joy for jealousy. I am peaceful and well-balanced in mind."

What you have gained, now give to others.

Think of all your near and dear ones, individually or collectively, and fill them with thoughts of loving-kindness, and wish them peace and happiness.

Now think of all beings living near and far, men, women, animals and all living beings in the East, West, North, South, above and below, and radiate boundless loving-kindness, without any enmity or obstruction, towards all, irrespective of class, creed, colour or sex.

Think that all are your fellow-beings in the ocean of life. You identify yourself with all. You are one with all.

Repeat to yourself: "May all beings be well and happy", and wish them all peace and happiness.

At the end of your meditation resolve that in the course of your daily life, you will try to translate your thoughts into action as the opportunity occurs.

Devotional Life, No.43, supplement to *Faith and Freedom*, No.97, Autumn 1979.

The Meditations of Marcus Aurelius

If you were of a sudden asked
'What hides within your mind?'
Could you, with perfect truth, reply
My thoughts are kind?

The souls of all take on the dye
And hues of daily thought,
So ever contemplate the good
The wise have taught.

Seek not for quiet in the hills
Or solitary place,
Tumult or peace within the heart
You there can trace.

Return within, the fount of good
Lies hidden in the soul
That inner centre where the truth
Abides in full.

Dig deep wherein there lies the well
Of all the good we know,
For ever dig, and that same spring
Shall ever flow.

Beneath the surface you must look,
See through the false veneer,
Intrinsic quality respect,
True worth revere.

With deity to shape your thought
And fill with love your mind,
Let this alone be your delight
To serve mankind.

Paraphrased in verse from *The Meditations of Marcus Aurelius.
Devotional Life*, No.44, supplement to *Faith and Freedom*, No.98,
Spring 1980. Also in *The Unitarian*, No.924, December 1980.

Meditation on Silence

The mind is nourished by darkness and silence.

Pliny the Younger

The Universe is very beautiful, yet it says nothing. The four seasons abide by a fixed law, yet they are not heard. All creation is based upon absolute principles, yet nothing speaks.

Chaung Tzu

Speech is of time, silence is of eternity.

Thomas Carlyle

Silence is wisdom, but the man who practises it is seldom seen.

Arab proverb

Speech was given to man to conceal his thoughts.

Voltaire

Silence is the mother of truth.

Disraeli

Silence does not make mistakes.

Indian proverb.

The tree of silence bears the fruit of peace.

Arab proverb

*   *   *   *   *   *   *

WORDS TO CLOSE SILENT MEDITATION
Our prayers are ended
Our thoughts are still
May we know peace and joy
This day and always.

Devotional Life, No.50, supplement to *Faith and Freedom*, No.104, Spring 1982.

BUDDHISM

Ten Buddhist Perfections

May I be generous and give,
(Dana — Generosity)

May I be pure and nobly live,
(Sila — Morality)

May I leave thoughts of self behind,
(Nekkamma — Renunciation)

May I seek wisdom till I find,
(Panna — Wisdom)

May I with vigour always act,
(Viriya — Energy, vigour)

May I be patient and have tact,
(Khanti — Patience)

May I be truthful as one should,
(Sacca — Truthfulness)

May I determine to do good,
(Adhitthana — Determination)

May I endeavour to be kind,
(Metta — Loving-kindness)

May I attain a balanced mind.
(Upekkha — Equanimity)

The Universalist, No.51, October 1997.

An Introduction to Buddhist Teaching

About the dates of the Buddha's life there is still some controversy, but it seems reasonably certain that he was born in 563 B.C., left home when he was twenty-nine, attained enlightenment when he was thirty-five and passed away in 483 B.C. at the age of eighty. His birthplace was Lumbini Gardens near Kapilavastu, the capital of the Sakya kingdom in northern India where his father, Suddhodana, was Raja. The child was called Siddharta, the family name being Gotama. "Buddha" is not a name, but a title which was only bestowed on him later in life after his enlightenment.

The boy Siddharta led the normal life of an Indian prince under the protective care of an anxious father, who, recognising in the boy an unusual degree of sensitivity, took every effort to keep from his eyes all knowledge of worldly woes. At sixteen — not an early age for marriage in ancient India — Siddharta married the beautiful Yasodhara, who later presented him with a son, Rahula For some time his life of princely ease continued, but then one day, driving forth from the palace, he saw an old man, then a sick man, then a dead man, and upon asking his charioteer at the sight of each what was the meaning of what he saw, was told, "This comes to all men." The he saw a recluse with shaven head and a tattered yellow robe. "What man is this?" he asked, and was told it was one who had gone forth into the homeless life. Then follows one of the most beautiful passages in Buddhist scriptures, indeed in the whole of literature:

> "He returned to the palace, deeply pondering, and, that night, while his pleasure girls lay sleeping in unbecom ing postures at his feet, he revolted from sensual pleasures, and at the same time the flame of compassion awoke within him. Not for the first time, but now with overpowering effect, he felt the positive call to save not only himself but all mankind from birth in the world of suffering. He bade farewell to his sleeping wife and babe, and in the silence of the Indian night went forth with Channa, his charioteer, and Kanthaka, his stallion. At the edge of the forest he alighted, cut off his long black hair with his sword and sent it back

to the palace by the hand of Channa. He exchanged his princely robes with those of a beggar and went forth into the homeless life, alone."

For six years or so that followed the Buddha-to-be subjected himself to the most rigorous spiritual and ascetic practices known to the ancient world. It availed him nothing. At last, emaciated almost to the point of death, he again took normal meals to regain his strength, and sitting beneath a Pipal tree — ever after known as the Bo-tree or tree of enlightenment — he resolved to remain in a state of meditation until he had found the answers to his questions. It was here that he received his 'enlightenment', so that for ever after he would be known as the Buddha — or 'enlightened one'.

What was the Buddha's 'enlightenment'? It was not a revelation from God, but a body of truth that he arrived at by his own strenuous mental effort. He did not think of himself, nor was he ever thought of, as God or even the Son of God. He was a man, a 'self enlightened one', a teacher. But what was his teaching? In a nutshell we may say that the essence of his teaching can be found in what are known as the 'four noble truths'. The Four Truths are these:

(1) All life is suffering.
(2) Suffering is caused by craving or desire.
(3) Suffering can be cured by stopping the craving.
(4) The Eightfold Path is the road that leads to the destruction of craving.

Before coming to the Eightfold Path a brief comment is called for on the first two Truths. Buddhism is by no means a joyless religion, and the Buddha was always the first to recognise that there is much in life that brings true happiness. Nevertheless sorrow and suffering are part and parcel of life and come to us all to a greater or lesser degree. To millions of people sorrow and suffering are the common conditions of life. It is obvious too that desire or craving is a major cause of suffering. There is nothing more frustrating than to desire something which we cannot have. And even if our desire is satisfied we do not find peace, for when one desire is satisfied another arises. True peace only comes with the overcoming of all desire. . .

The Eightfold Path

. . . We now turn to the Noble Eightfold Path, the treading of which leads to an end of craving and sorrow. As one would suppose, the Eightfold path has eight steps, though they are meant to be taken simultaneously. They are as follows:

(1) Right understanding (or belief). We must have at least an elementary grasp of the basic facts governing our lives before we can begin the spiritual life.

(2) Right thought or motive. Our thoughts must be pure and our motives honourable.

(3) Right speech. We must abstain from falsehood, slandering, harsh words and frivolous talk.

(4) Right action. Negatively this means we must refrain from harming others in any way whatsoever. Positively it means doing all we can to help others.

(5) Right means of livelihood. We must not earn our livelihood in any way that is injurious to others.

(6) Right effort. This means we must be discrimin-ating and give our energies to worthwhile ends.

(7) Right mindfulness. This means having constant mindfulness with regard to body, feelings, thoughts, and mind objects.

(8) Right concentration (or meditation). This means having one-pointedness of mind. It involves the constant practice of meditation.

The Noble Eightfold Path is the 'Middle Way' which all Buddhists should walk, between the extremes of licence and luxury on the one hand and asceticism on the other. To help them there have been laid down five Moral Precepts which all earnest Buddhists should strive to observe. These are:

(1) To refrain from injury to living things.

(2) To refrain from taking that which is not given.

(3) To refrain from sexual immorality.

(4) To refrain from falsehood.

(5) To refrain from liquor or drugs which engender slothfulness.

An introduction to Buddhist teaching, taken from *The Buddhist Festival of Wesak* [the Buddhist New Year] published in *Faith and Freedom*, No.68, Spring 1970.

The Power of Thought

The ability to think, the power of thought, is man's greatest gift. It is thought which moulds civilization and which has created many of the things we take or granted. As a tiny seed can produce a beautiful flower, as a small acorn can produce the mighty oak, so can thought produce the most wonderful things. Every book ever written, every symphony ever composed, every temple ever built, every scientific discovery ever made, every religious or political system ever created began in the mind of a man as a thought. Religion, philosophy, art, science, politics, and all the things we mean by civilization began as a thought. Among the religions of the world it is in Buddhism that the power of thought is given the strongest emphasis. The *Dhammapada*, one of the best known of Buddhist scriptures in the West, begins with the words:

"All that we are is the result of what we have thought: it is founded on our thoughts and made up of our thoughts."

And later it reminds us:

"The wise man shapes himself."

The creative or destructive power of thought — for it can indeed work both ways — has been known to the East for centuries. In the West we seem to have come to the discovery rather later, but our psychologists now tell us that many of our ailments are due to wrong thought. So worry, for example, is one of the major causes of ulcers, while fear, anger, hatred, and the constant dwelling on lewd thoughts, all take their toll. The same is true in the moral realm. Evil thoughts, constantly entertained, weaken the character and make one more susceptible to temptation. All evil words and deeds are preceded by evil thoughts, and evil thoughts — if allowed to remain unchecked — will lead eventually to evil words and deeds.

The surest way of keeping evil thoughts at bay is to discipline the mind to think constantly of that which is beautiful, true and good. When the mind is full of that which is good, the evil will seek for an entry in vain.

And the choice is important, for, as the *Dhammapada* again reminds us,

"If a man speaks or acts with an evil thought, pain follows him, as the wheel follows the foot of the ox that draws the carriage . . . . If a man speaks or acts with a pure thought, happiness follows him, like a shadow that never leaves him."

Dharma World, Vol.16, September 1976.

*   *   *   *   *   *   *

Temptation

Rain breaks through the ill-thatched dwelling,
Sound roofs keep the tenants dry.
Ill-trained minds give way to passions
Which the well-trained minds defy.
Let a man resist temptation
Like a city fortified,
Evil wreaks a cruel vengeance
Once it sets its foot inside.

Adapted from the *Dhammapada*.

The Unitarian, No.893, May 1978.

The Psychological Barrier

It has always seemed to me that Buddhists have cause to be grateful that they have never followed the example of their Christian friends in deifying the Founder of their religion. To deify one's Teacher is to transfer him to another plane where one cannot hope to follow. What relevance has the example of any great Teacher to us if he was essentially different from us? God — or a god — can be worshipped, he cannot be emulated.

Buddhists do not worship the Buddha, but try to do what is more difficult — follow his example. They recognise that if he lived such a good life AS A MAN, then there is no reason why they should not succeed in living good lives too, for they realise that the difference between the Buddha and ourselves is not a difference in kind but a difference in degree, and that there is hope that even we can follow where he has led. If the Buddha, as a completely normal human being, having known the full range of human experience from the sensuousness of Oriental palace life to the rigours of ascetic discipline, could by his own unaided efforts find the way to Enlightenment then so may we.

Many titles have been given to the Buddha out of reverence — but not worship — for him. I do not know that he has ever been called the Great Revealer, but that essentially is what he is, for he reveals our possibilities to us.

Men no longer regard it as impossible to climb Everest, or to run a mile in four minutes. In the same way we can no longer regard as impossible the life of utter self-forgetfulness, the life of compassion and purity, of nobility and virtue, the life of high endeavour and moral excellence. We can no longer regard as impossible the hope of finding Enlightenment. The Buddha has shown that it can be done, that it is within the realm of human possibilities. The psychological barrier is down. The way is clear for us to follow.

Extract from THE PSYCHOLOGICAL BARRIER published in *The Middle Way, Journal of the Buddhist Society*, Vol.45, No.2, August 1970.

"Freedom of Thought"

Buddhism does not cling to doctrine for doctrine's sake, and of all religions it is the least dogmatic. The Buddha Himself greatly admired intellectual honesty and was insistent that no one should do violence to his conscience by professing to accept anything which he could not really understand or believe. As He said:

> "Do not accept anything on hearsay. Do not accept anything by mere tradition. Do not accept anything just because it accords with your scriptures . . . But when you know for yourselves then do you live acting accordingly."

One should follow the Teaching, not blindly, but after examining it and finding it to be wholesome and certain to be beneficial.

This should not be taken as a licence for unbridled and determined scepticism, nor as permission to alter the Teaching to suit oneself. As Dr. Rahula has rightly commented:

> "Buddhism is not a belief or a faith in an imaginary god or divinity, to whose will you surrender all human responsibility. It is faith in man, it gives full responsibility and dignity to man, and thus makes man his own master, and rejects the false belief that there is a supreme being that sits in judgement over his destiny."

That is to say, the world is what you and I want to make of it, and not what some other unknown being wants to.

> "One is one's own refuge, who else could be the refuge?"

said the Buddha. He was always admonishing his disciples to observe this.

It is this spirit of freedom of thought, tolerance and understanding which is one of Buddhism's most cherished possessions. It is the reason why Buddhism has never been forced upon others by bribes, persuasion or the sword.

Further extract from *The Buddhist Festival of Wesak* published in *Faith and Freedom*, No.68, Spring 1970.

Cherry Blossom

In the Spring the Japanese have a charming custom known as viewing the cherry-blossom. People will travel many miles to see a famous cherry tree at its best, and some cherry trees are as well known as national monuments. People picnic beneath the trees, photograph them, paint them, praise them in haiku and drink large quantities of sake in their honour. For a few days the whole populace seems to be in the grip of cherry-blossom mania, and where real blossom is scarce, as in the cities, paper substitutes are made to serve instead.

There are several lessons we can learn from the cherry-blossom. Coming in the Spring it reminds us of the eternal cycle of rebirth. Lasting so short a time it helps us to remember the impermanence of all things. But it should not be forgotten that the blossom could not exist at all were it not for the roots of the tree buried deep in the ancient soil. Without roots no plant can live, nor any flower flourish.

In his Penguin book on Buddhism, Christmas Humpheys describes Zen as "the unique flower of Buddhism". But a flower needs roots, and as Christmas Humphrey's statement implies, Buddhism provides the roots from which the flower of Zen has grown and from which it continues to be nourished.

To try to understand Zen — if indeed such a thing is ever possible — without a reasonable knowledge of the roots from which it has grown in surely folly. Yet this folly is all too common in the West where Zen — or what passes for Zen — is in danger of becoming a fad among people whose knowledge of basic Buddhist philosophy is almost non-existent. To study the basic ideas of Buddhism is therefore the first task of anyone seriously interested in Zen.

There is one more lesson we can learn from the cherry blossom. The falling of a petal is natural and unpredictable — it just happens! If the Satori experience (the moment of Zen intuitive awareness) ever comes to us, it will come in the same way.

Extract from *The Zen Path to Inner Power* (unpublished manuscript).

Teaching and Parables

Like Jesus, the Buddha had that rare gift of being able to get to the heart of the matter and of putting things in such simple language that "the common people heard him gladly".

On one occasion a group of wandering philosophers became noisy about their several views. On hearing of the disturbance the Buddha gave a parable:

"A Raja sent for all the blind men in his capital and placed an elephant in their midst. One man felt the head of the elephant, another an ear, another a tusk, another the tuft of its tail. Asked to describe the elephant, one said that an elephant was a large pot, others that it was a winnowing fan, a ploughshare, or a besom. Thus each described the elephant as the part which he first touched, and the Raja was consumed with merriment."

So it is that each of us can grasp one aspect of the truth, but few can grasp the whole.

On another occasion two princes were about to do battle over a certain embankment constructed to keep in water. Upon being informed of the cause of the dispute the Buddha put the following questions:

'Tell me, O Kings, is the earth of any intrinsic value?' 'Of no value whatever,' was the reply. 'Is water of any intrinsic value?' 'Of no value whatever.' 'And the blood of kings, is that of any intrinsic value?' 'Its value is priceless.' 'Is it reasonable,' asked the Buddha, 'that that which is priceless should be staked against that which has no value whatever?'

The angry princes saw the wisdom of this reasoning and abandoned their dispute. If only we could get this wisdom across to world leaders today!

From the many examples of the Buddha's compassionate concern for even the weakest and the worst of men one will perhaps suffice as an illustration. In a place called Vaisali there lived a rich courtesan named Ambapali. Like many of her kind she cared only for money and pleasure, and hearing that the

Buddha was in the neighbourhood decided to flaunt herself before Him in order to insult Him. She was met with such a gentle, compassionate look that she became humble and begged Him to accept food from her. This He readily agreed to do in spite of severe criticism from others, who thought it unbecoming that He should accept an invitation from 'that mango-girl' as she was called. Ambapali became a convert and thereafter gladly walked the Noble Eightfold Path. None was too worldly or too low for Him to help.

On another occasion of great tenderness, Kisagotami, a young girl half-crazed with grief, brought her dead child to the Buddha for medicine. He agreed to heal the child, if Kisagotami would fetch him a grain of mustard. But there was one condition. The mustard had to come from a home where none had died. Kisagotami went from house to house, and all could give her a grain of mustard, but none from a house where none had died. Always the reply to her question was the same: 'Alas, the living are few but the dead are many. Do not remind us of our grief.' And so Kisagotami, putting aside the selfishness that made her think her grief exceptional, became a disciple of the Buddha and found comfort in comforting others.

Here is a practical approach to bereavement which we can commend to anyone regardless of their belief or disbelief in life after death. No one is alone in his grief, and comfort comes to those who comfort others.

One of my favourite parables is that of a man who came to a river he desired to cross. Finding no bridge or ferry he made himself a raft and safely crossed to the other side. But having found the raft of such use he refused to leave it behind and carried it with him on his back through forests and up mountains, whereupon it became a hindrance and not a help.

So does the Buddha illustrate that religious teaching is not an end in itself but only a means to an end, and that anything can be jettisoned when it becomes a hindrance rather than a help.

Further extract from *The Buddhist Festival of Wesak* published in *Faith and Freedom*, No.68, Spring 1970.

A Prayer

O Thou that art the Unborn, Unoriginated, Unformed,
in contemplation of thy eternal changelessness we see that
all else is but a transient manifestation of Thy Reality;
that the past is like a dream, the future a mirage,
and the present but a passing cloud.

Based on words attributed to the Lord Buddha.

*   *   *   *   *   *   *

The Wheel

Turning, ever turning,
   the world, the seasons and the Wheel
   to which I'm bound by chains of my own making.
Returning, ever returning,
   again and yet again to wear out bodies
   like suits of clothes and fill a thousand
   graves with useless bones.
Is there no end to this,
   no way to find the bliss of Liberation?
I will unyoke the chariot, make the stallions flee,
   and from the halted Wheel at last break free..

From *The Zen Path to Inner Power*, (unpublished manuscript).

*   *   *   *   *   *   *

A Prayer

O Turner of the Ceaseless Wheel, that bringeth all seasons
in their time, help us to see that as when the day's work is ended,
night brings the benison of sleep, so death is the ending of
a larger day, and in the night that follows every man finds rest
until he returns to fresh endeavour and to labours new.

(Incorporating words from *a Buddhist Funeral Service* published by
the British Buddhist Society.)

Lotus Blossom

Mud, slime, and from the gloom
Triumphantly a perfect bloom
Breaks through to greet the sun.
And we are taught the Way that saves,
The Path to tread,
That we may raise above the waves
A lotus-head.

The Inquirer, No.7338, 30 April 1994.

*   *   *   *   *   *   *

Work out your own salvation with diligence.

And so it was that at the age of eighty in a grove near Kusinara
his life came to an end. Serene to the last, he continued to in-
struct his disciples till his dying breath. Comforting his beloved
disciple Ananda, and reminding him that all men must die, he
exhorted his followers with the words:
"Work out your own salvation with diligence".
They were his last words.
He was cremated, and his ashes were spread
throughout the land.

Final extract from *The Buddhist Festival of Wesak* published in *Faith
and Freedom*, No.68, Spring 1970.

SAYINGS OF LI-SHU-K'UNG

The Way of Inner Peace

As a leaky vessel can never be filled, so can a greedy person never be satisfied.

He who has great wealth also has great worry. Only the treasures of the heart are safe from others.

Happy is the person who has a heart at rest from self.

Events hurt us less than we hurt ourselves by our attitude to them.

Be generous in your judgment of others, if you would wish them to be generous in their judgment of you.

A wise person neither over-estimates their own importance, nor under-estimates their own true value.

Happiness is like the desert mirage spoken of by travellers. Those who grasp at it find that they have nothing but a handful of sand.

Seek happiness and it will elude you. Give yourself to your duty with a quiet mind, and happiness will steal upon you unawares.

NATURE and ECOLOGY

A Prayer

O Energizer of the Universe, thou Creator Spirit and Sustaining Power, we remember in thy presence this world which is our home, and rejoice in the beauty and bounty of Nature.

We stand in awe before the rich variety of plant and animal life brought into being through the ages by the strange mysterious power of evolution.

May we learn to appreciate the wealth of beauty all around us, and to realize our responsibility to preserve it for future generations.

And so may we learn to order our community that the works of man shall not efface the works of Nature.

The Inquirer, No.6671, 23 May 1970.

The Ultimate Reality

Many years ago, taking a walk on the cliffs at Sheringham, I was halted in my tracks by the magnificent spectacle of the sun making its majestic descent into the sea. It was the most beautiful sunset it has ever been my privilege to witness, and as I watched that breathtaking sight the thought came to me again — as it had come many times before — that it would be utterly impossible to describe such an experience to a blind person. What words would you use to describe a sunset to a blind person?

The thought came to me too that we have the same problem when we try to describe or define God. I do not think it can be done, and I do not think we should even try. We all need more humility in talking about that Ultimate Reality we call 'God'. We should seek not to impose a definition but to show a way of life and demonstrate a religious discipline that can lead to a personal experience — a discipline that involves not only ethical endeavour but also the practice of regular prayer/meditation. For me the value of religion is in this, that it shows us the path which, if faithfully followed, leads to a personal experience of the Divine.

When the experience comes one can only bow down in speechless reverence. On returning to our holiday flat I sat down and scribbled in the back of my diary some words which eventually became the following poem:

Sunset

Evening in Sheringham
walking the cliffs,
skies reddened,
no breeze stirred,
no bird sang.
The sun set on a silent world.
What beauty for the eyes,
what treasured memories for the mind.
A thought occurred —
how could one tell the blind
of such rare gifts,
with what poor words describe the changing shades,
the sea's reflections,
as the rays are caught?

A deeper thought as sunlight fades —
the power behind the sunset's glow?
Life-Force, or Universal Mind,
no creeds reveal,
no church can show,
for 'God' can never be defined.
Only experience can know
what words can't tell,
With inward eyes at last we find
that which is Ultimately Real.

The Inquirer, No.7344, 23 July 1994.

Far Memory

Moonlight on water,
Beauty's perfection left its reflection
Mirrored in my heart.
The stream flowed on
And yet,
I did not forget
That haunting scene which was to be
So lastingly a part of me.

From *Zen Path to Inner Power*, (unpublished manuscript).

*   *   *   *   *   *   *

The Falling Leaf

I paused to pick up the leaf which had just drifted down at my feet. I will not attempt to describe it. To catalogue its tints and colours would convey nothing of its poignant beauty — a beauty which soon would linger only as a fading memory. How many leaves had the parent tree shed over many autumns? Yet one has read that no two leaves have ever been — would ever be — exactly the same. It was an awesome thought.

I held it lightly in my fingers with a sense of wonder and reverence which I have seldom had in church. A sudden gust snatched the leaf from me, and it went to join the anonymity of the autumn carpet which was forming all around. The spell was broken.

Yet for a few brief moments all the miracle and mystery of the universe had been caught for me in that one leaf. More than words could ever do, its dying beauty spoke to me of that which is undying — the creative life which is infinite and everlasting. With a feeling of humility, which I am ashamed to confess is all too infrequent, I silently gave thanks for the unearned joy of being alive.

The Inquirer, No.7403, 26 October 1996.

Wise cousins from the sea

One can generally estimate the intelligence of a creature by the weight and complexity of the brain in relation to the rest of its body. On this basis it has to be said that the dolphin brain is at least equal to the human one, and scientific observation of dolphin behaviour also suggests a very high level of intelligence. There is good evidence, for example, that dolphins have a system of communication which is as sophisticated as human speech, and they are able to have real 'conversations' with each other on quite complex subjects.

But to me the really endearing thing about the dolphins is not their intelligence, which I do in fact accept, but their gentle and friendly nature. In spite of the cruel way they have often been treated by humankind, there is no recorded cases of a dolphin ever attacking a human, though there are many well authenticated accounts of dolphins saving humans from drowning.

Dolphin

Locked in your complex brain
What thoughts lie hidden there,
If we could learn your speech
What secrets might you share,
What wisdom would you teach,
What knowledge might we gain?
We fill each day with care,
Our worries never cease,
What shall we eat, and wear?
How shall we keep the peace?
You who are truly free,
Playing with carefree mind,
Wise cousin from the sea,
Pity us humankind.

The Inquirer, No.7395, 6 July 1996

Chinese Morning Hymn

Golden breaks the dawn:
Comes the eastern sun
Over lake and lawn —
Set his course to run.
Birds above us fly,
Flowers bloom below,
Through the earth and sky
God's great mercies flow.

As the spinning globe
Rolls away the night,
Nature wears her robe
Spun of morning light.
Dawn break in me too,
As in skies above:
Teach me to be true
Fill my heart with love.

Hymns for Living, 1985, Number 279. First verse from Chinese of T.C.Chao, b.1888, tr. by Frank W. Price and Daniel Niles. Second verse J.A.S.

*   *   *   *   *   *   *

Benediction

When the sun sets in the western horizon
All labour is laid aside, men sleep,
The world is in silence.
How excellent are Thy designs,
O Lord of Eternity,
From whom cometh our rest and peace.

From *Akhenaton's 'Hymn of Aton"*.

Tomorrow's Harvest the Green Hope

There are those who doubt the value of the traditional harvest festival now that most of us live and work in towns and cities and so few are actually employed on the land. They argue that such Services are unreal for most of us, and therefore meaningless and irrelevant. They could not be more wrong! Anything which reminds us of our ultimate dependence on the world of Nature is of immense value, and few things do this more effectively than a traditional Harvest Festival when the Church is decorated with fruit, flowers and vegetables. It is surely not without significance that in most places Harvest is still one of the best attended services of the year.

Never before in the history of the world have we needed so desperately to be reminded of our dependence upon Mother Earth. Never were Chief Seattle's words more relevant:

"Whatever befalls the earth befalls the sons and daughters of the earth. Man did not weave the web of life, he is merely a strand in it. Whatever he does to the web he does to himself."

Many fear that if this lesson is not learnt soon we may be heading for the final catastrophe — the destruction of our Planet as a place fit for human habitation. This danger is not as remote as we may care to think, and over the last fifteen to twenty years a number of organisations have come into being to try to avert this disaster. Most of these — like the Conservation Society and the Friends of the Earth — are non-political. The exception is the Ecology Party.

What is ecology? In a nutshell, we may say it is caring today about tomorrow. In the words of one ecology poster:

"We do not inherit the world from our parents — we borrow it from our children".

They are words which govern the Party's thinking on every issue. Most political parties put their faith in something called 'Growth'. But though economic growth may bring limited short-term benefits, in the long-term the result is likely to be disastrous. If you keep trying to make the balloon bigger it will eventually burst and you will be left with nothing. What we should be aiming for, according to Ecologists, is a sustainable, stable society, with an emphasis upon conservation, recycling and the use of natural renewable resources.

The Ecology Party is far from perfect. Some of its ideas will have to be abandoned. Many will have to be modified. Politically it has a lot of growing up to do. But it is saying something new, and behind the occasional naiveté there is a message we must heed if we are to ensure that there will always be a tomorrow's Harvest.

The Inquirer, No.7065, 1 October 1983.

*   *   *   *   *   *   *

"That we may walk fittingly"

SONG OF THE LOOM
Our Mother the Earth, our Father the Sky,
Your children are we, and with tired backs
We bring you the gifts you love.
Then weave for us a garment of brightness;
May the warp be the white light of morning,
May the weft be the red light of evening,
May the fringes be the falling rain,
May the border be the standing rainbow,
Thus weave for us a garment of brightness,
That we may walk fittingly where birds sing,
That we may walk fittingly where grass is green,
Our Mother the Earth, our Father the Sky.

Tewa Indian, New Mexico.

Canticle of Conservation

O Earth, you are surpassing fair,
From out your store we're daily fed,
We breathe your life-supporting air
And drink the water that you shed.
Yet greed has made us mar your face,
Pollute the air, make foul the sea,
The folly of the human race
Is bringing untold misery.

Our growing numbers make demands
That e'en your bounty cannot meet,
Starvation stalks through hungry lands
And men die hourly in the street.
The Eden dream of long ago
Is vanishing before our eyes,
Unwise, unheeding, still we go
Destroying hopes of paradise.

Has Evolution been in vain
That Man should perish in his prime?
Or will he from his greed refrain
And save his planet while there's time?
The choice is ours, and we must say
Whether or not we will survive,
There is no time now to delay
If we're to save ourselves alive.

The Inquirer, No.6783, 20 January 1973.
The Good Earth, December-January, 1974-75.
As *The Choice is Ours* in *Hymns for Living*, 1985, Number 206.

SAYINGS OF LI-SHU-K'UNG

The Way of Man and the Way of Nature

Blame not Nature for the meanness of Her gifts, but man for the excesses of his demands.

As the gifts of Nature are for everyone without discrimination, so should the good person be all-embracing in their kindness.

In what way should people show their gratitude for the beauty of Nature? Is not the best way by trying to match the outward beauty of Nature with an inner beauty in their own hearts?

Man reaps the fruits of his behaviour as the farmer reaps a harvest from the seed he has sown. The consequences of his deeds will come back to him as surely as chaff cast into the wind returns to the thrower. This is the eternal law of Nature. Let all men take heed.

Men ask concerning the foundation of the earth and the beginnings of the human race. This is fruitless speculation. More important than the manner of our coming is the manner of our behaviour. We should strive to endow life with meaning rather than seek the meaning of life.

A CALENDAR

Stocktaking

In the great business of living we need our times of stocktaking, and at no time is this more appropriate than at the beginning of a new year. It is a time for questions, a time for reflection. What use have we made of the year that has gone? What mistakes have we failed to avoid? What opportunities have we failed to grasp? Less depressingly, what good have we done? What joys have we known? What love and fellowship have we shared? We each bring our own answers to these questions — our own thanksgiving or regrets.

One thing we all have in common. None of us can turn the clock back. The past is past — gone beyond recall. Gone are all the good times and the bad, the pains and pleasures, the heartaches and the happiness. Only the memories remain. Now we look to the future — made wiser perhaps by all that has gone before. Learning from the past, but not living there. We do well to listen to St. Paul, who advises us to forget the past and:

". . . to reach forth unto those things which are before."

Well, too, to take seriously the humorous words of Mark Twain, who in his wise and witty way tells us:

"We had better be concerned about the future, because that is where we are going to be spending the rest of our lives."

To live in and for the future — that is the challenge which comes to each one of us. For it is in the future that we shall find our hopes and opportunities, our chances to do a little better — to climb a little higher.

The Inquirer, No.7356, 7 January 1995.

Look both ways

Our pagan ancestors may have been very bad theologians, but they were often sound psychologists, and some of the insights enshrined in their myths we neglect at our peril. One of my favourite gods from pagan antiquity is Janus, the two-headed god who was able to look in two directions at the same time.

It was appropriate that January, the first month of the year, should be named after this god, for this is a time for looking both backwards and forwards. Some religions seem to be entirely backward-looking, and have become hide-bound, lacking any real vitality. Some, like the new American sects which seem to be concerned solely with the literal Second Coming of Christ and the end of the world, spend all their time looking towards some messianic future and lack the deep roots and stability that a sound tradition and historical background provide. Unitarians must learn to avoid these two extremes and, like the pagan god of classical mythology, look forwards and backward at the same time. We must always learn from the past, but we also need a vision of the future towards which we constantly work.

When we do look back, what a pity it is that we remember with gratitude only those whose names are famed in the annals of history. Yet there were others whose achievements were no less great. Who kindled the first fire, made the first wheel, built the first hut? Who built the first raft, scratched the first picture on a cave wall, sang the first song, told the first story? No one knows, yet their achievements were surely as great as any that we have seen in historic time. In a sense they were greater, since they were literally starting from scratch, and had it all to do. We have just added a few more bricks to the temple of knowledge. They laid the foundations.

The Inquirer, No.7382, 6 January 1996.

Human Love in The Bible:
Some thoughts for Valentine's Day

The little book commonly known as the *Song of Solomon*, or *Song of Songs*, was for many years regarded as an allegory. To the rabbis, it was all a picture of the mutual love of God and Israel. The Christian fathers took over this view and simply changed it to a picture of Christ and the Church, which appears as the Bride.

All allegorical interpretations should be set aside at once. The main reason the allegorical explanation was used in the first place is that much of the book is plainly about love, and the love intended is plainly the passionate love of a man and a woman. Even in pre-Christian days this was too much for some people in respectable society. The view that the book is an allegory is not seriously held today. Most scholars have at last come to the conclusion that this is a collection of love poems, which is what we all thought to begin with!

If it seems strange to find this book in the Bible, it is because of our preconceived notion of what the Bible ought to be. We tend to think of religion as one compartment of human life, one section all by itself, with its own peculiar words and actions and its own special day of the week. We do not understand what even quite primitive people realize, that if there is such a thing as 'religion' at all, it does not mean one rather odd bit of our lives, but a way of living all life. A religion which is worthwhile should permeate all our human experiences.

The Song of Solomon is almost in the middle of the Bible. That in itself is an allegory if that is what you want: human love is near the heart of religion.

The Inquirer, No.7384, 3 February 1996.

Lent:
A time for Spring-cleaning

A few weeks ago when I wrote a piece for the New Year I called it 'Stocktaking'. The same title could as well apply to this piece on Lent, for this is a time when we also need to take stock. On reflection I decided to call it 'Spring-Cleaning', for this is what Lent always means to me. It is a time when we have to examine our habits and our attitudes, a time when we should really make some effort to 'clean up our act'.

In the Christian tradition it is the time when we remember when Jesus fasted for forty days and forty nights in the wilderness. Many Christians try to give up some luxury or pleasure in Lent in remembrance of Jesus. Unitarians, as a rule, are not given to this practice, but it has a value. It is a useful exercise in self-discipline and can sometimes lead on to lasting benefits. I have known people who have given up smoking for Lent and have gone on to kick the habit for good. That is something I really applaud.

We know from our readings from the Scriptures that Jesus often sought times of solitude and silence in order to refresh himself spiritually and to strengthen himself for the work ahead. Even those Unitarians who do not call themselves Christians would do well to follow his example here. We all need to replenish our spiritual energies, to renew our strength. Such times can help give us a new perspective on life. "We need times of silence", wrote W. E. Orchard, "not to escape from life, but to find life more fully. We cannot see the work we are doing unless sometimes we stand back from it." An oil painting can only be appreciated when we stand back far enough to view the whole canvas. So too with life.

A real sense of the Divine Presence, spiritual refreshment and strength, and a sane balanced view of life — these are just some of the things which can be ours. Lent, far from being a time when we give things up, can be a time when we make gains which will greatly enrich our lives. I have no hesitation in wishing you all a happy Lent.

The Inquirer, No.7360, 4 March 1995.

Sacrifices

We all know that Benjamin Franklin, the great American states-
man, philosopher and scientist, was a Unitarian, but perhaps not
everybody realizes that among his many interests was an enthu-
siasm for chess. He saw it as a microcosm of life, and the playing of the game as a good training for daily living. Among his
many published writings is a little work called *Morals of Chess*
from which the following extract is taken:

"The Game of Chess is not merely an idle amusement; several very valuable qualities of the mind, useful in the course
of human life, are to be acquired and strengthened by it, so
as to become habits on all occasions. For life is a kind of
chess, in which we have points to gain, and competitors or
adversaries to contend with, and in which there is a vast variety of good and ill events that are, in some degree, the effects of prudence, or want of it. By playing at Chess then
we may learn: 1st Foresight . . . 2nd Circumspection . . .
3rd Caution."

Life has many analogies with chess. Fellow enthusiasts will
know that in the game there are gambits and sacrifices in which
a player will gladly accept the loss of material in the interests of
some long term strategy. To sacrifice a powerful piece like the
queen may sometimes look like suicide, but it can often open the
way to a dramatic win.

In life too there are sacrifices, and there have always been
those who are prepared to make sacrifices — even the ultimate
one. We think of Unitarian martyrs like Michael Servetus, John
Bidle, and Edward Wightman — the last man to be burned alive
in England for heresy. We think of great figures of the twentieth
century who placed their lives on the line by espousing unpop-
ular causes. Men like Mahatma Gandhi and Martin Luther
King, both of whom fell to the assassin's bullet, as they had
foreseen they would.

Now Easter will soon be with us again, and this is the time
when Christians think of, what is for them, the most celebrated
sacrifice of all — the death of Jesus. His message was never
popular with the authorities, and in spreading it he pursued a

dangerous path which he himself knew could lead to only one end. But people are more easily slain than ideas, and his spirit was too big for any grave. The message lives on, and perhaps all the more forcibly so because of the sacrifice which has become its most enduring symbol.

We shall, one hopes, never be called upon to make the ultimate sacrifice for our faith, and I for one have no wish to be a martyr. But in a small way we must all make sacrifices for the cause, or causes, which are precious to us. Sometimes we may wonder if it is all worthwhile and may have doubts about the outcome. But faithfulness and courage give us the promise of victory.

And when it comes it is sweet, like the exciting win I once had when I captained our local team in the Wirral League and, greatly daring, I sacrificed my queen!

The Inquirer, No.7362, 1 April 1995.

* * * * * * *

Easter
May we, too, arise and walk in newness of life

The festival we celebrate at this time of the year is one of great antiquity, pre-dating by many centuries the Christian era. As long ago as 735 CE, the Venerable Bede suggested that the word came from an Anglo-Saxon goddess called Eostre. Others suggest that it comes from the old Norse word Eostur — or Ostar — which meant the season of the rising (growing) sun, the season of new birth. The word was used by our ancestors to designate the 'Feast of New Life' in the spring. The word 'ost' meant east. The word Easter, then, originally meant the celebration of the spring sun which had its birth in the east and brought new life upon earth.

However the word Easter originated, there is no disagreement as to the original purpose of the festival. It was to celebrate the return of spring and new life after the dead days of winter. For our ancestors, winter was not simply inconvenient

and unpleasant, it was a struggle between life
which, all too often, death won. All this being th
surprising that they greeted Easter — the return c
with such universal joy. For them it literally spel
resurrection of new life.

Science and technology have cushioned our lives against
the worst severities of winter. Our lives now are so artificial, so
far removed from the world of nature, that the passing of the
seasons arouses in us little more than mild interest. Yet, though
we are seldom aware of it, we are still ultimately dependent on
the world of nature. In the last analysis the return of spring is as
vital to our survival as it was for the survival of any of our fore-
bears. Basically, we are as dependent on the return of spring as
were they. In comparison with them we show but little gratitude.

Yet surely our hearts must be dead if they are not capable
of being uplifted by the first signs of spring. Who has not been
stirred by the sight of the snowdrops, the crocuses and daffodils.
I like words of William Sullivan:

"Spring touches the shrivelled grass, speaks her creative
word to the naked trees, lets her footstep rest on the wasted
garden, breathes on the buried seed. And from the iron grip
of winter bursts the answering glory of leafage and verdure,
bud and blossom ripening for human needs, and flowers beyond all human speech."

And well might the author of Canticles sing:

"The winter is past . . . and the time of the singing of the
birds is come."

For me the message of Easter is the message of a new beginning. This is true of the life in trees and flowers, and it is yet
more true of the life of human beings like ourselves. What is
the distinctive thing about the human being? Surely this: that
she/he has a special capacity for making new starts. Easter, the
time when earth undergoes its annual resurrection, is surely a
good time for the resurrection of some of our old hopes and ide-
als. It is a time for new beginnings.

May we, too, arise and walk in newness of life!

The Inquirer, No.7336, 2 April 1994.

Whitsuntide
The real birthday of the Christian Church

Whitsuntide has often been described as the real birthday of the Christian Church, for it was on that first Whit Sunday, the Day of Pentecost, that the disciples found the courage to leave their place of hiding and proclaim their message to the world. We all know now just what this decision meant in terms of the suffering that came to them in consequence. Yet their faith never wavered, and they believed themselves to be inspired by the Holy Spirit — a Spirit they had first felt on the day of Pentecost.

In orthodox theology the Holy Spirit is the Third Person of the Trinity, but unlike the Father or the Son is very difficult to define. Even orthodox Christians tend to speak of the Spirit as an 'It' rather than a 'He'. A former Dean of St. Paul's, W. R. Matthews, was honest enough to write: "The New Testament evidence for a personal conception of the Holy Spirit is mixed, and I cannot resist the conclusion that, in many cases, the Holy Spirit is thought of as a power, influence or presence of God."

Significantly, many modern Christians find it less difficult to believe in the Holy Spirit than in the Father or the Son. Even in orthodox circles there is a growing tendency to think of God as a creative spirit — the 'Ground of our Being' — than a personal deity. Many who can no longer take literally the idea of the Fatherhood of God, or the deity of Jesus, still give credence to the notion that there is a divine energy at work in the world. Even George Bernard Shaw, who often described himself as an atheist, believed in the Holy Spirit, though he preferred to call it the 'Life- Force'. Someone — I forget who — once said that he/she regarded the Holy Spirit as the sole survivor of the Christian Trinity. That was perhaps an odd way of putting it, but many modern thinkers believe that the concept of Holy Spirit, or Life Force, will still be tenable long after all other ideas of God have been abandoned. If this proves to be the case, then Whitsun will not only be with us for a long time to come but may even grow in importance.

The Inquirer, No.7366, 27 May 1995.

Harvest thoughts

A radio programme some years ago coined the popular catch phrase: "The answer lies in the soil'. Urban dwellers — as most of us now are — need to be reminded that the answer does indeed 'lie in the soil'. Ultimately we are dependent on the gifts of Nature and the produce of the good earth. Do we, I wonder, look after the earth as well as the earth looks after us?

There is a harvest for the eyes and ears, as well as for the mouth and stomach, for we have been given more than the bare necessities of life. Not just bread and butter, but bread and buttercups! Flour and flowers! Moreover these 'extras' are free. How much did you have to pay to listen to the nightingale? Or watch the sunset? Or look at the rainbow?

There is of course a sombre side to the harvest season with its uncomfortable reminder that "as we sow, so shall we reap". As in the physical world, so also in the moral and spiritual:

> *Can the selfish reap contentment,*
> *Or the self-indulgent health?*
> *Can the indolent glean knowledge*
> *Or the idle gather wealth?*

Sombre thoughts indeed on which to dwell as we dig the produce from our gardens.

One final thought. Above all else the harvest challenges our sense of brother/sisterhood. How fairly do we share the resources of the world? As Mahatma Gandhi reminds us:

"The earth has enough for everyone's need, but not enough for everyone's greed."

From those who have received so much, much is expected.

"Freely ye have received, freely give."

The Inquirer, No.7375, 30 September 1995.

Good digging, and a Happy Christmas

It is a curious fact that many rationalists share with the funda-
mentalists the assumption that everything in the Bible is meant
to be taken literally — the only difference being that the funda-
mentalists believe everything, while the rationalists believe
nothing! Even Unitarians are sometimes prone to this error,
though they ought to know better!

The problem arises from the fact that the Bible was never
intended, initially at any rate, for prosaic Western minds. It was
written by orientals for orientals. Eastern peoples have an approach to truth which is quite different from ours, and when we
consider those of ancient times the difference is even greater.
How much of the Bible was intended to be taken literally is open
to question. I suspect very little, but we should not fall into the
opposite error of assuming that everything can be interpreted on
an allegorical basis.

I am one of those who take the Bible seriously — which is
not at all the same thing as taking it literally. Over the years I
have learned to take nothing in the Scriptures at face value, but
as I have dug beneath the surface I have found profound truths
to enrich and enlighten me which are not immediately apparent.

These reflections have been prompted by the approach of
Christmas when we shall again be confronted with the Nativity
stories. How do you view these stories? If you have failed to
see that they belong to the poetry of religion then you have
missed the whole point. If you are one of those who likes to call
a spade a spade, then you should use your spade to dig a little
deeper! You may be surprised and delighted with what you
find. Good digging — and a happy Christmas.

The Inquirer, No.7381, 23 December 1995.

The Mother

Did shepherds really come?
The magi from afar?
Or was it in her heart alone
That angels sang
And flamed a star?
Forget the song,
The fabled scene;
The grace of heaven
Was gently shown
By her love given.
For her, not Word fulfilled,
The god of creed;
He was her helpless child,
And she — his need.

The Inquirer, No.7276, 14 December 1991.

*   *   *   *   *   *   *

Star-led

Did the Lord of heaven and earth
Move a star across the skies
To announce the holy birth,
Guide the footsteps of the wise?

Greater wonder would it be
If God moved the stubborn heart
Till we bend a reverent knee
And from foolish ways depart.

Hallowed myths and treasured tales
Wisely used still have their place,
But their inner purpose fails
If we fail to grow in grace.

The Inquirer, No.7381, 23 December 1995.

PEACE

In this age of warring madness,
In this century of strife,
Was the face of pity hidden
That we failed to cherish life?

Mercy, were you there at Flanders
Or our bloodbath on the Somme?
Were you there at Nagasaki
When we dropped the atom bomb?

You were there, your gentle pleadings
Fell on ears grown deaf with pride,
Hatred reigned and blood-lust triumphed,
Hearts were stone and pity died.

Love constrain us, guide us, train us,
Purge all hearts until wars cease,
Make us one in true compassion
And compatriots in peace.

Green Songs, Evergreen Press, Bristol, 1983.

Never again

In his autobiography *Fen Boy First*, my brother Edward describes me as "a gentle pacifist from the day he was born." If that is true — and it may be — that may be one of the reasons why I have mixed feelings at this time of the year. As a minister I always observed Remembrance Sunday, but my emphasis was on peace and reconciliation. I tried to get people to remember all those who have suffered due to wars, not just the military, and not just the British military. Germans had their grievous losses too, and in common humanity we should remember them as well. I often think that the only real enemy is war itself.

Yet sadly the occasions that should bring out our finer feelings so often bring out our worst. It seems as though that has always been the case. After the First World War, many people, particularly ex-service people, were angered by the jingoistic 'victory banquets' and 'victory celebrations' which were organized. In 1925, Dick Sheppard (later to found the *Peace Pledge Union*) wrote to *The Times* to protest at the custom of holding a Victory Ball in the Albert Hall on Armistice Day — "not so much irreligious as indecent." The Festival of Remembrance, which evolved from 1927 onwards, promoted by the British Legion, incorporated an acceptance of militarism and military values which has continued to this day.

The feeling that something was very wrong with official events which too often glorified war, and seemed to be part of the preparations for the next war, was expressed eloquently in a *Peace News* editorial of 1937:

"What are we celebrating? Is it the death of brave men? If so all the days of the year are anniversaries of that event. Is it the magnitude of the tragedy? If so, what if a greater tragedy should occur, would that obliterate this celebration? If so, where are the signs that we should not repeat it? Is it to commemorate the sacrifice for something real and lasting? If so what is that something? Because if we are celebrating sacrifice for its own sake, then we are being sadistic. Those who celebrated Armistice in 1919 believed that November

11, 1918, was more than a passing date in history. They felt that an epoch had come to an end . . . The conscience of mankind has been witness that we cannot celebrate war itself, however proudly we remember the dead. If, then, we are to keep the celebration of Armistice with any worthiness at all, assuredly it must be for the purpose of renewing our resolution of 'Never Again'."

Only once in a ministry of over thirty years was I invited to take the main part in a civic Remembrance Service. That was at Lincoln, the city where they make a big thing of the poet Tennyson. There is a magnificent statue of him outside the cathedral. He has never been my favourite poet but I chose some words from his poem *Locksley Hall* to end my address. They look to the future with an optimism which I confess I seldom have myself. Nevertheless they are words which I hope we shall all think about at this time of the year and try to make come true.

The Inquirer, No.7351, 29 October 1994.

*   *   *   *   *   *   *

Remembrance Day Address

When, following the Pelopennesian war, the people of Athens assembled to mourn their dead, their greatest orator, Pericles, reminded them that:

"The whole earth is the sepulchre of famous. men: not only are they commemorated by columns and inscriptions in their own country, but in foreign lands there dwells also an unwritten memorial of them, graven not on stone but in the hearts of men".

As we gather today by this War Memorial to remember the fallen in two World Wars, let us remember that it is not enough merely to look at their memorials in stone. We must try to rear the memorial afresh in our hearts; lest in the stone they should be forgotten.

As we think of our obligation to the fallen, what is going to be our practical, as well as our vocal and emotional response? At least it ought to be a time of resolution; a time when we wholly resolve that the dead shall not have died in vain.

It is for us, the living, to translate memorial tablet and triumphal arch into heart-throb and pulse-beat, into flesh and blood, ready to sacrifice for peace, willing to minister to peace, eager to serve peace — that peace, which James Oppenheim has said: "demands all of a man, his love, his life, his veriest self." And then he gives us his great words of challenge:

"Build, while there is yet time, a creative peace —
while there is yet time!
For if we reject great peace,
As surely as vile living brings disease,
So surely shall your selfishness bring war."

We remember the dead, but we have this Act of Remembrance not to glorify war, but to remember its horror and tragedy, and to resolve a solemn affirmation that we shall never let it happen again. It was not a pacifist, but Field Marshal Earl Haig himself, who said: "It is the business of the churches to make my business impossible." But making war impossible is not only the business of the churches. It is a task for people of all religions and of none.

Our own poet, Lord Tennyson, had a vision of the future where all would be at peace. As I leave you with his words, let us vow that we shall work to make his vision come true.

"I dipt into the future, far as human eye could see,
Saw the Vision of the world, and all the wonder that would
   be.
. . . the war-drum throbbed no longer, and the battle-flags
   were furl'd
In the Parliament of Man, the Federation of the World.
There the common sense of most shall hold a grateful realm
   in awe,
And the kindly earth shall slumber, lapped in universal
   law."

Remembrance Day Address, Lincoln, c.1973.

The Peace Prayer

Lead me from Death to Life,
From Falsehood to Truth

Lead me from Despair to Hope,
From Fear to Trust

Lead me from Hate to Love,
From War to Peace

Let Peace fill our Heart,
our World, our Universe.

Peace . . . Peace . . . Peace

Mother Teresa of Calcutta made the first public pronounce-
ment of this prayer [composed by Satish Kumar] in St. James
Church, Piccadilly in July 1981. The prayer was officially
launched at an interfaith service in Westminster Abbey at mid-
day on 6th August (Hiroshima Day).

The prayer is not addressed to any particular deity, and can
be used by people of all Faiths, or of none. Some may prefer to
regard it as a meditation, or as an act of positive thinking. I believe strongly in the power of thought and I believe the positive
thoughts of millions of people — all directed purpose-fully to a
common end — can do enormous good. So use this prayer daily, and do it with all the sincerity, faith and hope that you can
muster.

The Unitarian, No.940, April 1982.

HYMNS

The Larger View
(". . . in common quest.")

In their ancient isolation
   Races framed their moral codes,
And the peoples of each nation
   Trod their solitary roads.
Now the distances are shrinking;
   Travel, and the printed page,
All earth's many lands are linking,
   Spreading knowledge of each sage.

Now new times demand new measures,
   And new ways we must explore.
Let each faith bring its own treasures
   To enrich the common store.
Then no more will creeds divide us —
   Though we love our own the best —
For the larger view will guide us
   As we join in common quest.

Hymns for Living, 1985, Number 126.

Children of the Universe

Children of the human race,
Offspring of our Mother Earth,
Not alone in endless space
Has our planet given birth.
Far across the cosmic skies
Countless suns in glory blaze,
And from untold planets rise
Endless canticles of praise.

Should some sign of others reach
This, our lonely planet Earth,
Differences of form and speech
Must not hide our common worth.
When at length our minds are free,
And the clouds of fear disperse,
Then at last we'll learn to be
Children of the Universe.

Hymns for Living, 1985, Number 132.

The Living God

Down the ages we have trod
Many paths in search of God,
Seeking ever to define
The Eternal and Divine.

Some have seen eternal good
Pictured best in Parenthood,
And a Being throned above
Ruling over us in love.

There are others who proclaim
God and nature are the same,
And the present Godhead own
Where Creation's laws are known.

There are eyes which best can see
God within humanity,
And God's countenance there trace
Written in the human face.

Where compassion is most found
Is for some the hallowed ground,
And these paths they upward plod
Teaching us that love is God.

Though the truth we can't perceive,
This at least we must believe,
What we take most earnestly
Is our living Deity.

Our true God we there shall find
In what claims our heart and mind,
And our hidden thoughts enshrine
That which for us is Divine.

Hymns for Living, 1985, Number 35.

Reverence for Life

In life's complex web of being
    Each is fitted for its place,
Plants and beasts and all things living,
    Peoples of the human race;
But the balances of nature
    Exploitation has disturbed,
And all creatures she will nurture
    Only when this greed is curbed.

Dolphin leaping through the waters,
    Skylark over lonely fen,
Timid fawn in dappled forest,
    Hungry lion in its den,
Butterfly, the bee and flower,
    Each should have its chance to thrive;
Humankind, restrain your power
    And for wider kinship strive.

Hymns for Living, 1985, Number 250.

Far too long . . .

Far too long, by fear divided,
   we have settled with the sword
   quarrels which should be decided
   by the reconciling word.

Now the nations are united,
   though as yet in name alone,
   and the distant goal is sighted
   which the prophet souls have shown.

May, at last, we cease from warring,
   barriers of hate remove,
   and, earth's riches freely sharing,
   found the dynasty of love.

Singing the Living Tradition, 1993, Number 160.

Our Nation

Long ago they came in conquest,
Stayed to make this land their home:
Viking warrior and Norman,
Legionnaire from ancient Rome.

Jewish victims of men's hatred,
Huguenots both rich and poor,
Fled the lands of their oppression,
Finding here an open door.

From the continent of Europe
Came Ukrainian and Greek;
And from lands of past dominion
Hindu, Parsi, Muslim, Sikh.

Many peoples, many customs ,
Many new things all must learn;
Each can make a contribution
To the common good we yearn.

All our cultures now converging
Let us learn to understand;
Till in love we've built together
One great nation in this land.

Hymns for Living, 1985, Number 214.

Liberation

God our Father and our Mother,
Help us to respect each other,
Loving all as sister, brother.

Widen now your daughters' vision,
Break the shackles of tradition,
Let their skills find recognition.

Help your sons to be more tender,
Arrogance at last surrender,
Gentleness in them engender.

Barriers have been erected,
Sister, brother, been rejected,
Human needs too long neglected.

Love for love shall be requited
When these ancient wrongs are righted,
And your children are united.

Hymns for Living, 1985, Number 218.

In the spring ...

In the spring, with plough and harrow,
  farmers worked in field and furrow;
  now we harvest for tomorrow.

Beauty adds to bounty's measure
  giving freely for our pleasure
  sights and sounds and scents to treasure.

But earth's garden will not flourish
  if in greed we spoil and ravish
  that which we should prize and cherish.

We must show a deeper caring,
  show compassion to the dying,
  cease from avarice and warring.

So may we at our thanksgiving
  give this pledge to all things living:
  that we will obey love's bidding.

Singing the Living Tradition, 1993, Number 71.

The Fellowship of the Church

The Church is not where altar stands
  Within the hallowed walls,
But where the strong reach out their hands
  To raise the one who falls;
Not stately building, standing fair,
  Where people sing their creeds,
But fellowship of loving care
  Which serves all human needs.

The Church is not where ancient rite
  Is seen on Sabbath days,
But wisdom's constant beam of light
  To guide our common ways;
The Church is me, the Church is you,
  Not mortar, brick and stone;
It is with all who love the true,
  And where true love is shown.

Hymns for Living, 1985, Number 173.

A footnote on hymns

. . . In the nineteenth century the repetition of words, or parts of words, was common, either in order to fit a particular tune or because it was thought to heighten the effect. Sometimes the results were quite amusing. Here are a few of my favourite examples:

"Come down Sal, come down Sal, come down salvation from above. . ."

And this one for hypochondriacs:

"And take a pill, and take a pill, and take a pilgrim to the skies. . ."

Or this one for bird-lovers:

"My poor poll, my poor poll, my poor polluted soul. . ."

Or how about this one for cooks:

"Stir up my stu, stir up my stu, stir up my stupid soul. . ."

And my own favourite — a real maiden's prayer this one!

"Oh for a man, oh for a man, oh for a mansion in the sky. "

. . . Hymns have been one of the most important vehicles for religious instruction, and often a message can be put across more effectively in a hymn than in a sermon. As the great hymn writer Philip Doddridge once said: "I do not mind who writes the theology, so long as I can write the hymns."

It has been said that a visitor from a non-Christian land would learn more about the Christian Faith by reading through a hymn book than he could hope to learn by the study of all the learned books on theology. And someone — I can't remember who — put it even more forcibly when he said that if the Christian Church and all Christian literature, including the Bible, were to disappear for a thousand years, the discovery of one really good comprehensive hymn book would make possible the reconstruction of the Christian Faith in all its essentials. . .

Extracts from manuscript of address given before the Lord Mayor and Lady Mayoress of Plymouth on the occasion of the visit to the city by the Fox Junior High School, Chicago, in June 1981.

HAIKU

Haiku are exceedingly short poems which consist of only seventeen syllables, arranged in three lines of five, seven and five syllables. Within this tiny structure the poet seeks to evoke a response so that the reader participates in the poem and becomes aware of a certain mood or experience.

A Haiku is like "a finger pointing at the moon"; one should not look at the finger (poem) but at that to which it points. Thus does the Haiku reflect the spirit of Zen from which it originated. Of all the arts, according to the great scholar Dr D. T. Suzuki, it is poetry which comes closest to catching something of the spirit of Buddhism, and of all Buddhist poetry it is the Haiku that we most associate with Japan. Toshimitsu Hasumi describes Haiku as the summit of Japanese literature, a summit that it took nine hundred years of evolution to reach. He calls Haiku poets "priests of speech", and defines their work as "an unmediated expression of their soul's' commerce with the Absolute".

Many Haiku poems which are now available in English translation are finding an enthusiastic welcome far beyond their country of origin. Not only this, but now many Western poets are also experimenting with this traditional Eastern verse form.

Condensed from *Japanese Poetry: An Englishman's View*, in *Dharma World,* Vol.6, February 1970, and *The Zen Path to Inner Power*, unpublished manuscript.

Fifteen Haiku

Only a pink blush
  On the sky-line's icy cheek
    Tells me it is dawn.

Springtime renewal
  Morning dew-drop in the sun
    Transient jewel.

A bird on a twig
  Pecking off the infant buds
    Does not halt the Spring.

Blackbird on a rock
  Stands as still as a statue
    Denying he lives.

The seagull in flight
  Cleaves through the sky like a ship
    But leaving no wake.

The falling raindrops
  Help the sun to paint the sky
    With rainbow colours.

On a sunless day
  My sad body tries in vain
    To make shadows play.

The shadowless wind
  Bends the tender young saplings
    With unseen power.

The impartial wind
  Stirring the rival banners
    Mocks the men of war.

The distant horses
  Nibble at the horizon
    Making silhouettes.

Beneath the bare trees
  The dry leaves dance in the breeze
    Their autumn farewell.

The falling snow flake
  Kisses the palm of my hand
    Becoming a tear.

Behind dappled clouds
  The shy moon hides from my gaze
    Her naked beauty.

Only the moonlight
  Illuminating my path
    Takes away the dark.

The silver moonbeams
  Dancing upon my pillow
    Weave garlands of dreams.

The second and seventh Haiku appeared in *The Inquirer*, No.6715, 20 March,1971. The last Haiku was included in *Japanese Poetry: An Englishman's View, Dharma World*, Vol.6, February 1970. The remaining twelve Haiku were published together as *Haiku Poems* in *The Japan Society of London, Bull*. 60, February 1970.

SPEAKING OUT

Save the butterflies!

Butterflies need all the help we can give them. So much damage has been done to their natural habitat in recent years that their numbers have seriously declined. When I was a small boy and first became interested in butterflies they seemed to exist in huge numbers. Sadly that is no longer the case. There are currently fifty-seven resident native butterflies in Britain and most of them are at risk. Four species have become extinct this century, the most recent of these the beautiful 'Large Blue' in 1979. How many more must go that way? I fear the worst.

Does it really matter, and aren't there more important things to worry about? Well perhaps, but the world would be a poorer place without the butterflies. Of the many attractions the summer has to offer us, for me the sight of butterflies against a bright blue sky is one of the most precious.

The importance of butterflies lies not only in the fact that they are beautiful, harmless and rewarding creatures, but also because they are sensitive environmental indicators, showing by their presence that the countryside is healthy. When the butterflies disappear it will not only be very sad, but it will also be a great worry. Could it be that we shall follow them some day?

Condensed from article in *The Inquirer*, No.7372, 19 August 1995.

Ethnic cleansing

We seem to hear a lot these days about 'ethnic cleansing', so much so that we may be tempted to regard it as a new phenomenon, But that would be far from the case. Throughout history there have been cases of ethnic cleansing and genocide, or attempts at these evils. Quite recently we have had occasion to remember Hitler and his attempt to exterminate the Jews of Europe. Our VE celebrations were, in part, a thanksgiving that he failed in that.

We ourselves would never do anything like that, or so we like to believe, but would we? I have been watching that excellent series on television called *The Wild West* when our American cousins were shamefully engaged in their attempt at 'ethnic cleansing'. What they did to try to rid the country of the original inhabitants, the native American Indians, is too awful to contemplate. As a boy I was made to feel that Buffalo Bill was a hero, but he was an ecological disaster. Destroying the buffalo herds for which William Cody was largely responsible was just one of the despicable things that were done to destroy the Indian way of life and threaten their survival.

It didn't stop there. There were more direct attacks on the Indians, and not only on the men, some of whom were warriors, but on the women and children. One cavalry officer (they weren't all bad) was sickened by the sight of 'little children on their knees begging for their lives and having their brains beaten out like dogs'. Scalps of slaughtered Indians were exhibited to rapturous applause at Denver Opera House. Even George Sherman, one of the heroes of the Civil War who I had always thought was one of the 'good guys', wrote: 'We must act with vindictive earnestness against the Sioux, even to their extermination — men, women and children. Nothing else will do.'

In the end the Indians were not exterminated but their traditional way of life was forever destroyed. Efforts were made to suppress their culture, their languages and religions. Under pressure, some Indians became Christians, but it is now widely believed that they gave more than they gained, and those who are interested in ecology and the environment think that they have a lot to teach us. St. Francis, I am sure, would have approved.

Not all Americans gave the Indians a hard time by any means. The Quakers, as we know, were on very good terms with them, and the Unitarians and the Universalists (they were separate bodies then) have nothing to be ashamed about. These were among those who early recognized the spiritual worth of the Indian ways. It is fitting that in his Lenten Manual for 1968 *Intimations of Grandeur* Jacob Trapp included a prayer which I have used frequently over the years. To finish on a positive note I would like to remind you of this prayer:

> *Great Spirit, whose voice is heard in the stillness,*
> *Whose breath gives life to all,*
> *We come before thee as children*
> *Needing the help of thy strength and thy wisdom.*
>
> *Grant us to walk in beauty,*
> *Seeing the uncommon in the common,*
> *Aware of the great stream of wonder*
> *In which we and all things move.*
>
> *Give us to see more deeply*
> *Into the great things of our heritage,*
> *And the simple yet sublime truths*
> *Hidden in every leaf and every rock.*
>
> *May our hands treat with respect*
> *The things thou hast created,*
> *May we walk with our fellow creatures*
> *As sharers with them in the one life that flows from thee.*
>
> (After a Sioux Indian Prayer)

Thank you Jacob Trapp for sharing that with us, and our heartfelt thanks to the Sioux as well.

The Inquirer, No.7370, 22 July 1995.

Operating in Middlemarch

Back in the fifties when I was an operating theatre technician at Peterborough's Memorial Hospital, I was sometimes required to go to nearby *Middlemarch* to help with the operations in the hospital there. I did not of course call the town *Middlemarch* in those days. Then I called it Stamford, which is how it is named in all the atlases. But for me, and for many television viewers, now it will always be *Middlemarch*. When BBC scouts were scouring the Midlands for a suitable location to film the television adaptation of George Eliot's novel, they could scarcely believe their luck when they reached Stamford. They should have asked me, I could have told them. Stamford even resembles prints of 1830's Coventry — which was Eliot's model for the town of *Middlemarch*. I'm sure George Eliot would have approved of the BBC's choice.

It is the hospital at Stamford/*Middlemarch* that I am most familiar with. Stamford's hospital was build in 1828, around the same time as the new Fever Hospital in *Middlemarch*. It has fallen on hard times, and not only because I am no longer around to help! Both the children's ward and the maternity unit have closed in the past five years, and further cuts are threatened. Just what Dorothea Brooke or Dr. Lydgate would have said about that I can only imagine. What I say is unprintable, at any rate in a respectable paper like *The Inquirer.*

We hear a lot these days from certain people about the need to get 'back to basics'. Just what they mean by that I am not sure. Are they sure themselves? But there is one 'basic' that I do want to get back to, and that is the kind of NHS that I knew in happier days. What has happened to the Health Service in recent years fills me with dismay and anger. What do we think we are playing at? In all the higher religions the care of the sick is a top priority. 'Whosoever would wait on me, let them wait on the sick' said the Buddha. You don't need me to remind you that Jesus said the same sort of thing on many occasions. Perhaps it is time we started to take them seriously. Then perhaps we might save the Health Service, once the envy of the world.

The Inquirer, No.7337, 16 April 1994.

A Mecca for Peace

Tavistock Square in London has become something of a Mecca for pacifists and all lovers of peace. There you will find the hunched statue of a seated Gandhi which reminds us of his methods of non-violence which he practised with such courage and eventual success in India. Nearby is the cherry tree in memory of the victims of Hiroshima. This has attracted many visitors in this the fiftieth anniversary year of the dropping of the bomb, many of them Japanese. Also nearby is the memorial stone to conscientious objectors which was unveiled some time ago by Sir Michael Tippett, himself a life-long pacifist. The stone bears the inscription:

> *To all who have established and are maintaining the right to refuse to kill.*

It is often said that pacifists and COs are far too quick to surrender, and put up no resistance to an aggressor. That is far from the case. Refusal to fight with weapons is not surrender. We should not be passive when threatened by the greedy, the cruel and the tyrant. We should struggle to remove the causes of confrontation by every means of non-violent resistance available. I think that Mahatma Gandhi with his method of non-violent non-co-operation sets us an example. We should always be prepared to use spiritual 'weapons' and not only in war. Putting aside the physical sword does not mean that we should never 'fight' or put up resistance.

I trust the situation will never arise, but if it did I hope I would have the courage to die for my country. Likewise for my religion. But I would kill for neither. I have never been a conscientious objector and in fact served for three years in the RAF, albeit as a medical orderly. But now I hope I would have the courage, and initiative, to insist on the right *"to refuse to kill"*.

The Inquirer, No.7378, 11 November 1995.

REFLECTIONS ON CHILDHOOD

"The oddest gift I can recall, however, was the pair of boxing-gloves my younger brother John received when he was eight or nine. A gentle pacifist from the day he was born, it was unlikely that he would show any aspirations then for pugilism, any more than he would have seen himself as a scalp hunter when he was given a wooden axe carved with pride by my father who decided one year that a tomahawk was the most eagerly awaited gift his second son required."

"The kitchen was also where my father did our shoe repairs. He had his own cobbler's last and bought his leather from the shoe-repairer in our street. I watched him many times as he cut a piece of shoe leather down to size and put a dozen sprigs between his lips, just like a proper cobbler, then nailed the new sole neatly on to an old shoe. 'You needn't think you'll get a new pair', he'd say, 'until you've learned to look after these' My brother looked on ruefully, knowing that when I had outgrown these boots they would be handed down to him."

Extracts from *Fen Boy First* by Edward Storey.

The six essays below all appeared in *The Inquirer*, in the following issues respectively:

> No.7354, 10 December 1994.
> No.7331, 22 January 1994.
> No.7334, 5 March, 1994.
> No.7345, 6 August, 1994
> No.7348, 17 September, 1994.
> No.7328, 11 December, 1993

Of boxing gloves and tomahawks

It is perverse of me, I know, but I often find rebels oddly appealing. Perhaps this is why I enjoyed the following story which is found in a book I was given one Father's Day. A little boy was to have played the part of Joseph in the Nativity Play but was demoted to the innkeeper because he was so naughty. All went well on the day until Mary and Joseph rolled up at the inn and asked if there was any room: 'Masses of room for everyone', said the innkeeper blandly. 'Come in at once'.

The book I have just referred to is called *When We Were Young* and is a collection of childhood reminiscences from famous people. Not surprisingly many of the entries are about Christmas and predictably the book soon put me in a nostalgic mood.

I remember especially the Christmas when I was given a magnificent American Indian outfit , complete with feathered head-dress and tomahawk. My parents must have noticed that in my games of cowboys and Indians with the other boys I always insisted on being an Indian, and would never be a Cowboy. I am still very much on the side of the Indian! Another Christmas my most cherished present was a pair of boxing gloves. As my other interests at the time included reading and writing poetry, and collecting wild flowers, I needed to be able to box for my self-preservation. I was very good at it too - though I am ashamed to admit it now. A lasting passion for which I need offer no apology is chess, and I am still using the set I was given when I was about thirteen or fourteen. What a lot of pleasure that has given me over the years.

I have long since buried my tomahawk and hung up my gloves, but the joy they gave me at the time is still a pleasure to remember. I think memories are the most precious things we can give anyone. But memories need not concern tangible gifts. Laughter and tears, love and sympathy, warmth and understanding, these are the things I remember most. This festive season let us resolve to give each other happy memories through our shared friendship and our constant goodwill.

Ploughtime

Although the Nonconformist church which I attended when I was young always made a big thing of the harvest, and I mean BIG, it made very little of Plough Sunday. We left that to the Anglicans! As a boy, I envied my friends next door who went to the High Anglican church at the end of our street, where a plough was taken into the church to be blessed by the vicar. How I wished that my church would do something like that. But I don't suppose that any vicar ever blessed the plough which was used on Plough Witch Monday, which used to take place in my home town of Whittlesey when my father was a boy. A group of strong men would pull a plough round the town threatening to pull up people's doorsteps if they did not contribute a copper or two to their collecting-box. I suspect it was not an idle threat!

When I was at school, horses were still commonly used on the farms, and not least for ploughing. The magnificent shire horses, which seemed as gentle as they were strong, never failed to fascinate me and watching them ploughing was one of the delights of my childhood. Ploughing was a job that required patience and skill, and those who did it took a pride in their work. They needed always to look ahead, and always resist the temptation to keep looking back. Such was the pride of the ploughmen that there used to be 'ploughing competitions', with prizes for those who ploughed the straightest furrow. It is difficult now to remember that those events were almost regarded as 'spectator sports', and often created as much excitement as a Peterborough United cup match. After such a competition, the field with its rows of dead straight furrows looked almost like a work of art — which in a way it was.

Even as a child I was impressed by the care farmers took to cultivate their land, and if they had a good harvest it was no more than they deserved. Looking back now I often wonder why we don't take as much trouble in cultivating our own lives as the farmers do in cultivating their land. That could give us a rich harvest too.

Prize-giving

For most scholars the Christmas party was always popular, and the yearly outing to the seaside if anything more so, but for me better than either of these was Prize-Giving. This took place at a special service in March, and often a visiting preacher would address the children and present the prizes. Dutifully I tried to listen, but usually the words just washed over me. My mind wandered, and my thoughts kept turning to the books displayed so enticingly on the table before us.

After what seemed hours, but which could only have been minutes, the homily would come to an end, and the prize-giving would begin. Going forward to receive my book always produced mixed emotions in me. Being by nature a bashful child, I hated being the centre of attention, but nothing would have prevented me from claiming my prize. I would hardly dare look as it was handed to me. Would I like it? Would I be disappointed? Fortunately this was seldom the case. Once back in my seat with the prized book on my lap I would be lost to the world. For all the notice I took of those around me I might have been the only one there. I had my prize, and at that moment nothing else mattered.

In my church in those days the books we received were nearly always of a religious nature, but by no means dull on that account. When it came to excitement and adventure most compared favourably with my more secular reading. How I lived those stories! With Livingstone I explored darkest Africa. I braved the perils of the deep with the Pilgrim Fathers as they sailed for America. And in fear of my life I hid with early Christians in the catacombs of ancient Rome. I was, I suppose, what was called a 'fanciful child' and few things fuelled my imagination more readily than books. They were my 'Open Sesame' to a world of wonder and delight. More surely than any magic carpet the turning of a page could waft me to far away places and distant ages where adventure was always to be found.

In time I outgrew those books and the simple faith they reflected, but for me religion is still an adventure — an adventure of the mind and spirit.

Summer 'treats' and googlies

How delighted our Sunday School was after the war when we could once again go to the seaside for our annual summer 'treat'. During the war we had to make do with games in our local park, and we were lucky to have those. The only seasides within easy reach of our home town were on a not very interesting stretch of our coast. They were flat and featureless, and often cold from the North Sea winds. Not a bit like 'Sandy Bay' where Rupert Bear went for his holidays. There were no caves and rock pools, and I never once saw a pirate or mermaid.

Our seasides had one big advantage, however, their flat hard sands made perfect pitches for beach cricket. What games we had. The boys tried to emulate their heroes, much to the amusement of the girls. I tried to bowl googlies like my hero, Eric Hollies. You may remember he was the man who bowled Don Bradman for a duck in his last Test. But however hard I tried to take wickets, and impress the girls, I soon came to the conclusion that I would never be another Eric Hollies. Not until some years later when I went to college and switched to bowling off-breaks did I achieve any success in cricket. Then I took a hat trick for our college team and earned their admiration for the rest of the season. How I have bored my poor family with this account over the years.

Now the cricket season is in full flow, and I am having my annual bout of nostalgia. Perhaps I am just getting old, but the game no longer seems the same. This saddens me. What saddens me even more is that Sunday School trips to the seaside for beach cricket seems to be a thing of the past. What a lot of innocent fun we had, and what a lot we learned from our play, and not only about cricket. I am sure we were all a lot better for it — in more ways than one.

.

Bringing in the sheaves

The Carol Service was, of course, the high spot of the year in the life of our chapel, but the Harvest Festival ran it a close second. This was a 'three service Sunday' with a special service in the afternoon as well as the usual morning and evening worship. The afternoon service was of particular interest to the Sunday School, and we children looked forward to it with eager anticipation. Not for us the grown-ups' discreet and almost furtive bringing of harvest produce the day before. Our gifts were carried in splendid procession and received by the preacher at the front of the chapel.

Each year, two children, a boy and a girl, would be chosen to lead the procession, and each would be given a small symbolic sheaf of corn to carry. One year I was given this privilege. I must have been a little too young to appreciate the honour for, at first, I had to simulate the excitement my companion seemed genuinely to feel. As we led the procession into the chapel, the noise was almost overpowering, for the large congregation rose as one person and began to sing: "Bringing in the sheaves, bringing in the sheaves, We shall come rejoicing, bringing in the sheaves". No longer did I need pretend, for at that moment I felt more excited than I had ever been before. The singing moved me more than I would have thought possible, and I struggled to fight back the tears.

Suddenly I realised that what I was doing was tremendously important. It was my first deeply religious experience, and it left its mark indelibly upon me. As we reached the front of the chapel and I handed over my sheaf to the preacher, I sensed intuitively that the ritual in which I was participating was immeasurably ancient. No one had ever told me this, and I had certainly not gleaned the knowledge from my meagre reading. I simply knew, and knew with a conviction which was unshakable. And I was right too, as my studies in later years confirmed, for, from time immemorial harvest rites have been practised and this widespread observance transcends all barriers of race and creed.

Still today the Harvest Festival is one of the most popular services, and it is right that it should be so. If the desire to celebrate it is ever lost, then the future will be bleak indeed - not only for religion, but for the race itself.

A hand outstretched

As one reached adolescence, there were other attractions. Each year the youth club, with the assistance of a few brave volunteers from the chapel choir, would go out carol-singing to raise money for some good cause. I shall never forget the first year I was old enough to go. We had not enjoyed a very successful evening around the streets, and after much deliberation it was decided that we should sing outside *The Bull*, our local inn. There was so much noise going on inside, I felt sure that no one would hear us. But after a while someone must have heard for suddenly their revelries stopped and our voices alone rang out across the night sky.

Then a wondrous thing happened. Once more a great noise came from *The Bull* as the customers began to join in the singing. The friendly landlord — so unlike the innkeeper in the Nativity story — came to the door and invited us in out of the cold. This led to more debate, but greatly daring we eventually entered what for some was regarded as a 'den of iniquity'. I did not know quite what to expect, but certainly not this. The scene was straight out of Dickens, with a low timbered ceiling, now hung with paper-chains, and a roaring log fire. A darts match had just finished and Mr. Carter, the postman, was the hero of the moment, having just thrown the winning dart. He must have delivered his darts with greater accuracy than the mail, for the legend was that he could not read, so often were letters put through the wrong doors.

The euphoria arising from their celebrated darts' victory had put the patrons of *The Bull* in a generous mood, and our collecting tins were well and truly loaded by the time we left their convivial company. When we emptied our tins later that night we were jubilant, for the total far exceeded our expectations and we were able to make a really substantial donation to a Charity for the Homeless, our good cause for that year. And what better way to honour the birth of one who had 'no where to lay his head'. For surely this is the meaning of Christmas — not just candles and carols, crackers and cake, but caring and sharing and a hand stretched out in love.

SAYINGS OF LI-SHU-K'UNG

The Way of Virtue

Only the foolish expect to be rewarded for their virtuous behaviour. The wise person knows that the life of virtue is a reward in itself.

The wise man makes his body his slave. He does not become a slave to his body.

As a man's face is reflected in still water, so are the virtues reflected in the life of a good man.

Courtesy may not be the greatest virtue, but without it the others lack beauty.

He or she who knows compassion knows life, for what is life if not an opportunity for loving?

People should be judged not by their achievements, but by the use they made of their opportunities.

Many yearn for a long life, few yearn for a virtuous one. But it is not yours to choose how long you shall live, so why yearn after eternity when you have not yet learned to use wisely the few short hours of a single day?

EPILOGUE

The Eternal Now

The present slips into the past
And dream-like melts away,
The breaking of tomorrow's dawn
Begins a new today.
The past and future ever meet
In the eternal now . . .

The Unitarian, No.889, January 1978.

*   *   *   *   *   *   *

Longing

Oppressed by the world's sorrow
The sky makes changing shapes
To lighten my mood,
Brighten my hopes.
Against deepening blue
Pink clouds promise a good tomorrow.
May the promise come true.

The Universalist, No.45, October 1995.

A Sermon in Wood

Christmas already seems a long time ago, but I still haven't read all the books I was given. I have looked at them of course, and I can see that they will give me a lot of pleasure and much food for thought. But it is not only books that can give us food for thought. One of our joint presents was a fine wooden candle-stick, a product which had been turned from a beautiful mature tree. It would have bothered me if a tree had been chopped down to make it, but that is not the case. Many mature trees were uprooted during the devastating storms of October 1987 and January 1990. It was from those trees *The Woodland Trust* has commissioned woodturners to create beautiful products, and the sale of these products will raise funds for the trust so that they can plant more trees and protect our woodlands.

That something so beautiful and useful should have come out of something that at the time must have seemed a total disaster gave me food for thought. I was soon calling it a 'sermon in wood'. After all, if Shakespeare could speak about 'sermons in stones', why not a 'sermon in wood'? In the past I have seen occasions when something good has come out of bad or difficult situations, and I know people who, against all the odds, have made something of their lives, sometimes even something beautiful and praiseworthy. That is what we all should try to do.

The Buddha spoke of those who with skill 'shape their wood' and the fletchers who 'straighten their arrows'. He went on to say 'Wise people shape themselves'. Let us hope that my 'sermon in wood' will help and inspire me to shape myself.

The Inquirer, No.7386, 2 March 1996.

The Secret Pain

The secret pain, the heart oppressed,
The formless fears we cannot name,
The troubled dreams which haunt our rest,
The guilty thought, the sense of shame;
All these we bring, with fragile trust,
In half-held faith's uncertain mood,
Here may all anxious cares be lost
And courage found to tread life's road.

The Inquirer, No.7019, 6 February 1982.

*   *   *   *   *   *   *

The Secret Door

We journey down a private road
To share at last a common fate,
Where, at life's end, we shed our load
And, leaving all, pass through death's gate.

What lies beyond that secret door?
What unseen country waits us there?
What new dimensions to explore?
What fresh experience to share?

To travel on in ways unguessed
And down some unknown path to wend?
Or enter an eternal rest —
That dreamless sleep that has no end?

Or maybe in some future age
Once more inhabit mortal flesh,
And tread again this worldly stage —
Perform the ancient role afresh.

We cannot say, for none can tell,
What lies beyond this mortal span.
We only know it will be well
To make THIS life the best we can.

The Unitarian, No.957, September 1983.

Squirrel on my shoulder

In my last ministry at West Kirby and Chester I had to do some things I had not done for years, and that was to give children's addresses. There is, of course, printed material to help the preacher and the teacher; there are books of children's stories, and there are stories in the Bible which are suitable for children — even Unitarian children!

But the talk which I gave which got the warmest response did not come from any book, but from my own experience. It was a true story about one of my special friends, a furry friend with a bushy tail who lived in the park near my home. We used to meet quite openly when I took a welcome break from writing my sermon and slipped out for a little walk. This used to be the highlight of my day, and I think my friend felt the same way.

My friend would spot me soon after I entered the park and would run over to me straight away. If I stood quite still she would put her front paws on my feet and look up at me. She even ran up my walking-stick in an effort to get on my shoulder. A pirate will sometimes have a parrot on his shoulder, as I expect you have often seen, but how often have you seen someone with a squirrel on their shoulder?

The children were not the only ones interested in hearing about my friendly squirrel; the adults seemed to be interested as well, but it was the children who I asked to draw me pictures. I am often deeply touched by the Christmas cards which I receive, but never more so than by the card the children gave me after I had told them about my friendly squirrel. Instead of the usual robin or reindeer my card featured a magnificent squirrel. I left West Kirby a year ago having had to take an early retirement on health grounds. As a farewell gift the children gave me a beautiful pottery figure of a squirrel — ' to remind you of your friendly squirrel'. It is one of my most cherished treasures.

I often think of my friendly squirrel. And I shall never forget those friendly children.

The Inquirer, No.7355, 24 December 1994.

Four last Haiku

The winter passes
  Snow melts to feed the rivers
    And birds sing again.

Marigold garland
  Beauty with ugly intent
    Becoming a wreath.

Life's much-treasured gift
  The friendship we long to share
    To give and receive.

Lily in the grass
  Dwarfed beside the lofty pine
    But that too will pass.

Unpublished manuscript.

Astronomy lesson

Over the years one of the things I have looked forward to in the autumn, as some consolation for the end of the summer holidays, is the evening classes which start at that time of the year. I have done many things over the years, but one which I especially enjoyed was Astronomy. Much of it was over my head — which is where you would expect the stars to be — but on the whole it was fascinating and instructive. Even the little bit of the Universe we can observe contains billions of stars, and our own galaxy, the Milky Way, contains an estimated one hundred thousand million stars. In our class we were taught that there are known to be as many galaxies as there are stars in the Milky Way. That is a lot of stars!

So vast is the Universe, that although light travels at a constant speed of 186,000 miles a second, the light from the most distant stars visible to us has taken thousands of years to reach us. It is a strange thought, but when you look at the heavens you are seeing them not as they are now but as they have been in the past. Some of the stars we 'see' may no longer be there, although we are still receiving from them the light which began its journey in the distant past.

Going to evening classes often gave me ideas for sermons, not to mention hymns and poems. The thought came to me in my class, or perhaps when I got home, that some of the great men and women of the past are like stars whose goodness continues to shine and lighten our path though they are no longer with us in the flesh. In the words of one of my hymns:

'The lives of those who serve the right,
Shine with a lustre that will last.'

Perhaps the following poem says something of what I mean:

We're taught that stars — like people — die,
That what we see is just their light
Which travels on through endless days
Until it glimmers in our sky,
But though these suns no longer blaze
They still add lustre to our night.

The luminaries of this earth,
The saints, philosophers and seers,
Though dead, like burned-out stars in space,
Still shed a light across the years,
For though they share our common birth
They shine with more than common grace.

We too, though made of lesser clay,
May leave an echo of our stay.

The Inquirer, No.7349, 1 October 1994.

*　　*　　*　　*　　*　　*　　*

Love's Hope

Another age, another shore,
Incarnate in another frame,
My heart's true love I've known before
Though called by now forgotten name.
Together we again shall be,
For ties that bind our hearts remain,
My true love will return to me
And I will claim her once again.

From *The Zen Path to Inner Power*, unpublished manuscript.

The Power of Prayer

What place, if any, does prayer have in the lives of those who think of God as a Power, rather than a Person? Can we establish any meaningful relationship with a Deity that is other than personal? How does one pray to the Ground of Being?

I think the analogy of electricity may provide one answer. Electricity is an invisible force, though we are able to see some of its manifestations. We do not know exactly what it is, or fully understand how and why it works, yet from it we are able to derive great practical benefits. By plugging various appliances into this impersonal force we are able to obtain heat, light and power. In like manner by 'plugging in' to the great Life Force or Ground of Being — the Cosmic Energy which some call 'God' — we recharge our spiritual batteries.

'Nothing good can ever come to us except by our union with the creative energy of God', Emily Herman tells us in her book *Creative Prayer.* Becoming united with God — however conceived — is what religion is about, and prayer is the means of 'throwing the switch' which enables contact to be made. The language of prayer, whether or not it seems to be directed to a personal Deity, is relatively unimportant. There is something about prayer itself which seems to act as a switch to establish contact with the power we call God. 'Through real prayer', as F. C. Happold reminds us, 'a vast energy is generated which transforms, enriches and illuminates, for through it we are linking ourselves with that Power which is the inexhaustible motive force which spins the universe'.

But can such a Power actually answer our prayers and solve our problems? In his Gifford Lecture, *The Divine Flame*, Alister Hardy had an interesting suggestion:

> *Instead of supposing that one great personal-like Deity is thinking out simultaneously the detailed answers to millions of problems of all the individuals of the world, is it not more reasonable to suppose that some action is set in motion by prayer which draws the particular solution for each of us from our own subconscious minds?*

For me religion has always been a journey, especially an inward journey, and if there are any answers I am sure that is where they must be sought and found.

What we draw from within ourselves we can also radiate to others. I believe that in one of its aspects at least, prayer is 'consecrated telepathy' which is purposefully directed. Many of us have benefited from the prayers of others, even if we do not know exactly how it works.

Whatever theological changes take place, prayer will always have a value. As the physicist John Tyndall has told us so truly:

Often unreasonable, if not contemptible, prayer in its purer forms hints at disciplines which few of us can neglect without moral loss.

This, John Storey's last article, was published posthumously in *The Inquirer*, No.7434, 3 January 1998.

As each day ends

As each day ends, may I have lived
That I may truly say:
I did no harm to humankind,
From truth I did not stray.
I did no wrong with knowing mind,
From evil I did keep;
I turned no hungry soul away,
I caused no one to weep.

Hymns for Living, 1985, Number 302.   Adapted by J.A.S. from *The Book of the Dead*, Ancient Egyptian, c.2500 B.C.

Facing death

The wise and good should never dread
Whichever fate awaits the dead:
To live again or rest in sleep,
Gives no one any cause to weep:
So one may tread with footsteps brave
The path that leads one to the grave.

Hymns for Living, 1985, Number 297. Recast by J.A.S. after Socrates.

* * * * * * *

Tomorrow's past

We are tomorrow's past.
We cast a shadow,
write a page in history's growing tome.
In time to come
our own — this present age —
like ancient Greece and Rome shall disappear.
No throne can long endure,
each has its day — and all must someday end.
We are tomorrow's past,
unless, through folly, our today
becomes for all Mankind
the last.

From *Voices Seeking Peace*, Unitarian Peace Fellowship, 1990.

A LIFE

John Andrew Storey was born on 24th March 1935 at Whittlesey, Cambridgeshire, in the Isle of Ely. Home for his whole childhood and youth there was a modest two-up two-down terrace house, now demolished, in Church Street. Whittlesey lies between the two cathedral cities of Ely and Peterborough, nearer the latter, in the unique British Fenlands characterised by their extreme flatness and huge skies, and with a history of sturdy yeomen dissenters.

John was the third of four surviving children. The oldest, Edward, has provided an account of their family life in Whittlesey, rich in anecdotal material and implicit social comment, in his *Fen Boy First* published in 1992. It is clear that family life was warm-hearted but strict, and that there was very little cash to spare. Sundays were toyless and attendance at the Congregational church, twice at service and once at Sunday School, obligatory for the children. Their parents had met at its Sunday School and worshipped there all their lives.

While still at school John had joined the St. John Ambulance Brigade and when he was called up for national service, he elected to sign on for three years so that he could become a medical orderly in the Royal Air Force. After his discharge, he worked for six months in the operating theatre in Peterborough hospital. Although attracted to medicine as a profession, the call to the ministry was stronger, and he was to spend five years, 1956-61, training for the Congregational ministry at Western College in Bristol.

Course work at Western College was thorough. While there, John became very interested in the study of comparative religion. A determination to seek enlightenment from all sources, "universalism", was to become the leading theme in John's whole thinking, philosophy, and life.

For relaxation, John greatly enjoyed reading, music, and chess. He was wiry and strong, enjoyed walking, and both rowed and played cricket for his college, once achieving a hat-trick against an Oxford college. Towards the end of his college days he met and married Sylvia Richards.

John's first post was as Congregational minister (1961-63) serving a group of five churches centred on Stonehouse, Gloucestershire in the lower Severn valley near the present wildfowl centre of Slimbridge.

Then John took the radical step of leaving the Congregational ministry to become a Unitarian. Undoubtedly John was attracted by the liberal traditions of Unitarianism, including the freedom to seek truth from whatever sources, the use of reason to examine these truths, and tolerance for others' beliefs.

His first Unitarian ministry was in Stalybridge, Cheshire, (1963-66). After three years came a move to Lincoln. This was a busy, happy and extremely productive time for John and Sylvia and their growing family. One year John was invited to give the Civic Remembrance Day address in Lincoln — quite an unusual honour for a Unitarian in a cathedral city.

It was during this period that John began writing the hymns for which he is best known and for which he will surely be long remembered, His hymn-writing was initially triggered by a reaction to Enoch Powell's notorious "rivers of blood" speech in 1968. John was extremely concerned that, given potentially inflammatory comments from leading politicians and others, racist attitudes current at the time might become entrenched in British culture. He took positive action and joined the Lincoln branch of the International Friendship League.

Considering his output of hymns, as Eleanor Dixon has so perceptively observed, "Know his hymns and you know the man". They are sung today in many countries round the world, especially at interfaith services.

John's ongoing interest in comparative religion led to his becoming a founder of the Unitarian Buddhist Society in 1972. It is apparent that John's strongest interest outside the traditional Judeo-Christian framework came to lie in a Buddhist approach to spirituality, an interest that is well represented in the choice of material here.

After Lincoln, John became Unitarian minister in Plymouth from 1979 to 1984. During this period he found time to give practical expression to his concerns over racism, conservation, ecology, and peace. He stood as an Ecology Party candidate for both City and County Councils. In all these activities in Plymouth it is fair to say that John was in advance of general public opinion at the time but, along with others, did more than his share in shaping it. John also served for several years as a member of the Theological Panel of Unitarians.

Then followed his last Unitarian ministry, based in West Kirby and Chester. This should have proved a serene time for the Storeys but it came to be marred by the onset of symptoms of multiple sclerosis in 1987 when John was 52. John bore this cruel and progressive illness with dignity, fortitude, and acceptance. Instead of complaining "Why me?" as many of us might have been excused for doing in similar circumstances, John used to say "Why not me?"

My family and I also became residents of West Kirby at around this time and came to know John and Sylvia and their family. We also came to appreciate John's gifts as a minister: his deep spirituality, his fine and thoughtful sermons, his sympathetic response to those in trouble or grief, his gentleness. John was keenly aware of the benefits of meditation and liked to introduce periods of meditation into his services. Although John enjoyed a self-consistent body of beliefs shaped by his own endeavours, he was always characteristically very tolerant of others' opinions. Many indeed are those who could echo these observations.

It was with very great regret that John was forced by worsening health to take early retirement in 1994, when he and Sylvia went to live near Sherborne, close to the Dorset-Somerset border. During an all too short period of retirement John wrote a large number of articles and poems, rivalling, indeed surpassing in productivity his earlier years at Lincoln. Several of these are included here, notably in the sections *A Calendar, Reflections on Childhood,* and *Epilogue.* During this period John regularly met with the Religious Society of Friends, the Quakers, in nearby Yeovil and found the customary periods of silent worship in their meetings especially uplifting and inspiring.

John died in Yeovil hospital on 5th December 1997 aged 62. A funeral service, conducted by his friend Eleanor Dixon, Unitarian minister for Crewkerne, included organ music of Bach, two Storey hymns, and this reading from the Gitanjali of Rabindranath Tagore:

"I thought that my voyage had come to its end at the last limit of my power, so that the path before me was closed, that provisions were exhausted and the time come to take shelter in a silent obscurity.

But I find that thy will knows no end in me. And when old words die out on the tongue, new melodies break forth from the heart; and where the old tracks are lost, new country is revealed with its wonders."

The funeral service also included a moving tribute from John's son Jonathan, who spoke of the multi-faceted nature of his father, citing his heroism, humility, gentleness, strength, acceptance, great intellect, teaching skill, and unconditional love. John was indeed always very proud of his three children Jonathan, Alison, and Jeremy, and their achievements, and also very much enjoyed the company of his grandson Carl and step-grandson Kristian.

After his death there arose a spontaneous and strong feeling that a selection of his works and thoughts should be collected and published, so that they could not only be treasured but also shared with a wider audience. The undertaking of this work in 1999 was tragically to coincide with the sudden and premature death of Jonathan, who had so looked forward to seeing it in print.

John Storey never chose to be assertive, or to seek high standing, or attempt to be identified as a leader of a universalist trend, or anything of that nature. Rather, he simply chose to be guided by his conscience and his intellectual curiosity.

John Andrew Storey was not primarily a writer who happened to write about spiritual matters. Rather, he was a deeply spiritual man who yearned and strove to communicate. Whenever one reads his works, their great clarity and compelling sincerity is apparent. They also reveal a picture of a remarkably fulfilled, constructive, and unified life, one based on conscience and a series of forthright choices. His life was indeed a shared "Adventure of the Spirit".

UNITARIANISM

"A unique religious movement, distinctive in its freedom, its breadth of outlook, its focus on humanity, and its foundation of individualism . . ."

John Hostler

John Storey became and remained a Unitarian minister. Consequently there have been several references to Unitarianism in this book. Now it could well be true that whereas many Unitarians might come to read it, many readers may not be Unitarians. This appendix is intended primarily to provide some background information for the latter.

Arising from the radical Protestant Reformation in Europe and mindful of the teachings of Jesus, Unitarianism does not accept all traditional Christian doctrine and dogma. An attitude of honest questioning leads, among other things, to scepticism concerning the deity of Jesus of Nazareth and especially the Christian doctrines of the Atonement and the Trinity — hence the derivation of the name Unitarian. A more positive definition would be as follows:

> *Unitarianism is based on faith in man, specifically on man's conscience, man's reason, and man's will and ability to act freely as conscience and reason may dictate to him (or her) personally (the term man is of course here used inclusively for our species, humankind).*

So, the answer to the commonly asked question, "Well, what *do* Unitarians believe in?" is that Unitarians base their lives not on any *creed* but on the above *principle.*

This may come as a surprisingly novel concept to those accustomed to the familiar patterns of revealed religions, which incorporate, indeed tend to insist upon, a specific set of unchanging beliefs shared by all adherents. In contrast to this, individual Unitarians are free, indeed encouraged, to explore whatsoever may seem of interest and importance to them personally in all matters, whether these be of religion, philosophy, science, or whatever, using material from any source. This leads to the personal working out of religious ideas and principles, and to considerable diversity and discussion between men and women within the Unitarian movement.

Some Unitarians may not care to venture outside the great legacy of the teachings of Jesus and easily find enough inspiration in them to guide their lives. Others, like John Storey, who questioned the strict Christian faith he grew up with and instead discovered that "Our faith is but a single gem upon a rosary of beads", enjoy a universalist approach. Yet again, others may develop a great appreciation, love, and concern for the majesty of Gaia, God's creation on earth. Some of these may be led in turn to consider the spiritual links between man and nature, particularly as perceived by so-called primitive peoples, past and present. And some could be strongly motivated to take practical action in such fields as voluntary work and campaigns for social reform. And a great many Unitarians, again like John Storey, could well embrace some or all of each of the above in varying proportions in their philosophies and life-styles! Unitarianism does indeed confer an added bonus of flexibility in meeting new challenges in our changing world, notably today in environmental concerns and interfaith initiatives.

Looking at the British scene, we find that, after 17th century forerunners, when some of them suffered imprisonment for their beliefs, Unitarianism became well established in England in the 18th century and grew greatly in the 19th century. This growth was due, at least in part, to a gradual public acceptance of advances in natural science, which were seen to be at variance with Christian dogma, itself in part based on a literal interpretation of events described in the Bible. Priestley, Lyell, and Darwin subscribed to, or were sympathetic to, Unitarian principles.

So it was, too, with a large number of influential writers, including William Hazlitt, Charles Lamb, Charles Dickens, and Elizabeth Gaskell. Much of their work was calculated to arouse the social conscience of the nation. Unitarians were prominent in support of campaigns for the abolition of slavery, the Chartist movement, rights for the common people, universal suffrage and votes for women, among other issues.

Many relatively unsung Victorian Unitarians devoted themselves to social welfare and reform. If you go, for example, to any of England's great industrial cities and look around at the memorials in public buildings, parks and squares, you will see testament to those who strove and gave towards such practical things as free education, public libraries, hospitals, public health projects, safe water supplies and sanitation, and suchlike. Delve a little deeper and you will find that many of them were Unitarians. Of course they were not alone in promoting reform, but the fact remains that Unitarians played an influential role out of all proportion to their actual numbers at a critical time in the evolution of Britain, where the industrial revolution was being pioneered with some dire social consequences.

One of the reasons for concerns of this nature is the Unitarian emphasis on the sanctitiy of the individual and a belief that people are marred by circumstance rather than innate depravity or "original sin". Another reason is that Unitarianism leads one to focus one's efforts towards working for a better life in *this* world.

In the United States, we find that no fewer than five US Presidents were Unitarians: John Adams, Thomas Jefferson, John Quincy Adams, Millard Fillmore, and William Howard Taft. Clearly, the *Declaration of Independence*, whose words still stir the soul, owes not a little to the Unitarian idealism of its chief draughtsman. American Unitarians have also included prominent writers, philosophers, and inventors. Vance Packard has put the position thus:

> "The Unitarian Church, tiny in total number, outranks all denominations in the number of eminent Americans who have claimed it as their church."

Although Unitarianism is still relatively strong in Britain and America, it is also established in Europe, Canada, Australia, New Zealand, India, and elsewhere.

The guiding principles of Unitarianism, despite their obvious unpopularity with some religious establishments, reflect a legitimate and widely held approach to life. They belong to a noble tradition of rational inquiry into important matters of conscience and belief. One suspects that, despite living through the materialism and moral amnesia of the late 20th century, a surprisingly large number of people today, if pressed to think about and define their beliefs, might be found to be Unitarian at heart.

So, if you should ever come to ask, "How do I become a Unitarian?" or even "How can I find out more about Unitarianism?" the first answer, as Phillip Hewett once aptly pointed out, is that almost certainly you already are one! You could of course go on to locate your nearest Unitarian church, where you would find a real sense of community and fellowship, without any danger of brainwashing. In this age of alienation and anxiety, a feeling of fellowship and belonging somewhere is of considerable benefit, one could almost say vital, to the wellbeing of an individual. Many thinking people who may feel that they just do not "fit in" comfortably with faiths or sects that, for one reason or another, seem to make unreasonable demands on them, find themselves "at home" in Unitarianism.

It should be stressed that Unitarianism is tolerant of others' beliefs. It recognises the important part that established beliefs and practices may play in other people's lives and, like Buddhism, does not seek to convert. People from another faith or of none could go to a Unitarian service and should find nothing in it to offend them. They might notice some deliberate omissions, but equally they may discover new insights and new avenues for thought and action. The two things that a Unitarian would distrust and oppose are intolerance and bigotry; indeed, one can hardly fail to be aware of where these can lead in our world of today.

Probably the most important single thing that a Unitarian would value and encourage is education, bearing very much in mind the true meaning of the word — "to lead out" (from the Latin educare) — that is to say the development of individual potential. We may not all be Jeffersons or Darwins, but we each have a role to play and something to contribute as well as learn, as we each pursue our quest.

". . . For the person who wants to be told the answers to life's greatest questions it [Unitarianism] probably has few attractions; but for the person who wants to find them out himself or herself, it undoubtedly has many."

John Hostler

SELECTED BIBLIOGRAPHY

Chryssides, George: *The Elements of Unitarianism*, Element Books, Shaftesbury and Boston, 1998.

Chryssides, George (Editor): *Unitarian Perspectives on Contemporary Religious Thought*, Lindsey Press, London, 1999.

Hewett, Phillip: *On Being a Unitarian*, Canadian Unitarian Council, Toronto, 1976.

Hostler, John: *Unitarianism*, Hibbert Trust, London, 1981.

Houff, William H: *Infinity in Your Hand: A Guide for the Spiritually Curious*, Skinner, Boston, 1990.

Kereki, Gábor: *Unitarianism*, Lindsey Press, London, 1996.

Reed, Cliff: *"Unitarian? What's That?" Questions and answers about a liberal religious alternative*, Lindsey Press, London, 1999.

USEFUL ADDRESSES

Unitarian and Free Christian Churches,
  1-6 Essex Street, London WC2R 3HY, UK.
  Website: www/unitarian.org.uk
Unitarian Universalist Association,
  25 Beacon Street, Boston, MA 02108, USA.
Canadian Unitarian Council,
  188 Eglington Ave. E.,Toronto, M4P 2X7, Canada.